Blood Wedding, Yerma,
and *The House of Bernarda Alba*

García Lorca's Tragic Trilogy

TWAYNE'S MASTERWORK STUDIES

Robert Lecker, General Editor

Blood Wedding, Yerma, and The House of Bernarda Alba

García Lorca's Tragic Trilogy

DENNIS A. KLEIN

TWAYNE PUBLISHERS • BOSTON
A Division of G. K. Hall & Co.

Twayne's Masterwork Studies No. 71

Copyright 1991 by G. K. Hall & Co.
All rights reserved.
Published by Twayne Publishers
A division of G. K. Hall & Co.
70 Lincoln Street
Boston, Massachusetts 02111

Copyediting supervised by Barbara Sutton.
Book production by Janet Z. Reynolds.
Typeset by Compset, Inc., Beverly, Massachusetts.

First published 1991.
10 9 8 7 6 5 4 3 2 1 (hc)
10 9 8 7 6 5 4 3 2 1 (pb)

Printed and bound in the United States of America.

Library of Congress Cataloging-in-Publication Data

Klein, Dennis A.
    Blood Wedding, Yerma, and The house of Bernarda Alba : García
Lorca's tragic trilogy / Dennis A. Klein.
        p.   cm. — (Twayne's masterwork studies)
    Includes bibliographical references and index.
    ISBN 0-8057-8351-2 (alk. paper). — ISBN 0-8057-8144-7 (pbk. :
alk. paper)
    1. García Lorca, Federico, 1898-1936—Criticism and
interpretation. I. Title. II. Series.
PQ6613.A763Z7347   1991
862'.62—dc20   90-21521
                                                        CIP

Contents

Note on the References and Acknowledgments

I refer to the texts mentioned in this book by their original Spanish titles and by my own translations of those titles, as follows:

PROSE ·

Impresiones y paisajes　　　　*Impressions and Countryside*

POETRY

Libro de poemas	*Book of Poems*
Poema del cante jondo	*Poem of the Deep Song*
Primeras canciones	*First Songs*
Canciones	*Songs*
Romancero gitano	*Gypsy Ballads*
Poeta en Nueva York	*Poet in New York*
"Llanto por Ignacio Sánchez Mejías"	*"Lamentation for Ignacio Sánchez Mejías"*
Seis poemas gallegos	*Six Galician Poems*
Divan del Tamarit	*Divan of Tamarit*
Sonetos del amor oscuro	*The Sonnets of Dark Love*

Plays

El maleficio de la mariposa	*The Butterfly's Evil Spell*
La Niña que riega la albahaca y el Príncipe preguntón	*The Girl Who Waters the Basil and the Inquisitive Prince*
Los títeres de cachiporra: Tragicomedia de don Cristóbal y la señá Rosita	*The Billy Club Puppets: Tragicomedy of Christopher and Rosie*
Mariana Pineda	*Mariana Pineda*
Teatro breve ("El paseo de Buster Keaton"; "La doncella, el marinero y el estudiante"; "Quimera")	*Short Plays* ("Buster Keaton's Stroll"; "The Maiden, the Sailor, and the Student"; "Chimera")
La zapatera prodigiosa	*The Shoemaker's Prodigious Wife*
Amor de don Perlimplín con Belisa en su jardín	*The Love of Perlimplín with Belisa in the Garden*
Retablillo de don Cristóbal	*Christopher's Little Stage*
Así que pasen cinco años	*As Five Years Pass*
El público	*The Audience*
Bodas de sangre	*Blood Wedding*
Yerma	*Yerma*
Doña Rosita la soltera o El lenguaje de las flores	*Rosie the Spinster; or, The Language of Flowers*
La casa de Bernarda Alba	*The House of Bernarda Alba*
Comedia sin título	*Untitled Play*
Lola la comedianta	*Lola the Prankster*

All plays quoted in this book © Federico García Lorca's Heirs.

The playwright's proper surname was García; Lorca was his mother's maiden name. It is common for Spaniards to use both, with the father's name first. I shall generally refer to him as Lorca, the surname that he preferred, rather than as García Lorca, which would be correct in Spanish usage. I shall occasionally refer to him with familiarity as Federico, as is often done by his biographers.

Among the many fine critics who have written on Lorca are Profs. Vicente Cabrera, Luis González-del-Valle, and Sumner M. Greenfield, whose studies I refer to in the Notes and Bibliography. Professors Cabrera and González-del-Valle and I studied with and wrote doctoral dissertations on Lorca at the same time under the direction of Dr. Greenfield at the University of Massachusetts; we also studied together in his seminar on Lorca. We are all indebted to him for the solid foundation he provided us with and for teaching us how to approach Lorca's plays.

I am grateful to the libraries of the University of California at Los Angeles and the University of Chicago, as well as the New York Public Library, the Center for Research Libraries, and the Biblioteca Nacional in Madrid for allowing me to use their resources. I thank, too, the Interlibrary Loan Department at the I. D. Weeks Library of the University of South Dakota. Deep thanks go to the Board of Directors of the Bush Foundation/Faculty Development Program at the University of South Dakota for funds to travel to libraries and stay in New York and Madrid while I was conducting my research; to the administration of the University of South Dakota and the Board of Regents of the State of South Dakota for granting me a sabbatical leave; and to the Office of Financial Aid for providing me secretarial assistance.

I wish to express appreciation to the Mercedes Casanovas agency for allowing me to quote from the plays. My deepest thanks go to Doña Isabel García Lorca, Federico's sister and president of the Fundación García Lorca in Madrid, for graciously inviting me to her office and for offering her assistance with any questions or problems that I might have; and to Don Manuel Fernández-Montesinos García, the playwright's nephew and the secretary of the foundation (as well as to his secretary who is too modest to wish to be named), for their helpfulness and for permission to reproduce the photographs in this book.

Federico García Lorca.
Courtesy of the Fundación Federico García Lorca.

Chronology:
Federico García Lorca's
Life and Works

1898	Federico García Lorca is born 5 June in Fuente Vaqueros, a small town on the outskirts of Granada, Spain. His father, Federico García Rodríguez, is a wealthy landholder, and his mother, Vicenta Lorca, is a teacher who introduces her son to the joys of learning and of music. The poet has one brother, Francisco, who becomes a professor at Columbia University, and two sisters, Concha and Isabel.
1909	Federico's family moves to Granada, close to the Sacromonte area, where the gypsies of Spain live. Their caves will appear in *Bodas de Sangre* (*Blood Wedding*), and the gypsies themselves in *Romancero gitano* (*Gypsy Ballads*).
1914	In accordance with his father's wishes (and against his own inclinations), enters the University of Granada to study law; also takes lessons in piano and guitar. His association with his music professor, Martín Domínguez Berrueta, leads to the publication of Federico's first book, *Impresiones y paisajes*.
1917	Travels through Spain with Domínguez Berrueta.
1918	*Impresiones y paisajes* (*Impressions and Countryside*), which he dedicates to his music professor and other companions on the trip, is published.
1919	Begins his studies at the University of Madrid, where he lives at the Student Residence Hall ("*la Resi*"). During his stay in Madrid, which lasts until 1928, he becomes friends with the future artist Salvador Dalí and future film director Luis Buñuel. The three creative spirits have strong artistic influences on each other. Produces *El maleficio de la mariposa* (*The Butterfly's Evil Spell*), his first play for the stage; directed by Gregorio Martínez Sierra, the playwright of *Canción de cuna* (*Cradle Song*).
1921	Publishes his first book of poetry, *Libro de poemas* (*Book of Poems*), dedicated to his brother Francisco. His poetry and

commentary on his own work begin to appear in the Spanish periodicals *El Sol* and *Índice*.

1922   Along with composer Manuel de Falla, organizes a festival in honor of Granada's *cante jondo* (deep song) of Andalusian origin.

1923   Produces a puppet show of his play *La Niña que riega la albahaca y el Príncipe preguntón* (*The Girl Who Waters the Basil and the Inquisitive Prince*) for the children of Granada. Receives his degree in law.

1926   Publishers "*Oda a Salvador Dalí*" ("Ode to Salvador Dalí").

1927   Returns to the stage with the historical drama *Mariana Pineda,* his first collaboration with actress Margarita Xirgu; the stage settings are designed by Dalí. Enjoys his first success as a playwright. Thanks in large part to Dalí, has a showing of his drawings in Barcelona. The name of the Generation of 1927, of which Lorca is a member, derives from the homage organized in honor of the three-hundredth anniversary of the death of the Spanish baroque poet Luis de Góngora, at which Lorca reads his essay "*La imagen poética de don Luis de Góngora*" ("Luis de Góngora's Poetic Imagery"). Publishes *Canciones* (*Songs*), dedicated to poets Jorge Guillén and Pedro Salinas, among others.

1928   Publishes *Gypsy Ballads* and thus becomes an international personality. Also writes three one-act plays (which have come to be known as *Teatro breve* [*Short plays*]) in the surrealistic mode: "*El paseo de Buster Keaton*" ("Buster Keaton's Stroll"), "*La doncella, el marinero y el estudiante*" ("The Maiden, the Sailor, and the Student"), and "*Quimera*" ("Chimera"). The first two appear in *Gallo* (Rooster), a magazine he cofounded. The magazine dies after two issues; "Chimera" was scheduled to appear in the third number. Close friendship with Salvador Dalí ends.

1929   Sails to New York, where he enrolls as a student at Columbia University. Despite an active social life, he is lonely, a feeling reflected in the posthumously published collection *Poeta en Nueva York* (*Poet in New York*). Finds the city, except for Harlem, to be a cold and heartless place.

1930   After his withdrawal from classes at Columbia, leaves for Cuba where he lectures at the invitation of the Institución Hispanocubana de Cultura. Here he composes the poem "*Son de negros en Cuba*" ("The Sound of the Blacks in Cuba"), which later appears in *Poet in New York*. Returns to Madrid and

	stages *La zapatera prodigiosa* (*The Shoemaker's Prodigious Wife*) with Margarita Xirgu's theatrical company.
1931	Reads the poems that he wrote in New York at *la Resi*. Publishes the collection *Poema del cante jondo* (*Poem of the Deep Song*). Writes the puppet farce *Retablillo de con Cristóbal* (*Christopher's Little Stage*). Gives a private reading of *Así que pasen cinco años* (*As Five Years Pass*), a surrealistic drama that he wrote in New York. Alfonso XIII abdicates the throne of Spain, and the Second Republic is established.
1932	Cofounds (with Eduardo Ugarte) *La Barraca* (The Hut), a traveling theatrical troup that brings Spanish classics to the rural areas of Spain.
1933	Two scenes of the controversial drama *El público* (*The Audience*), which Lorca considers impossible to stage, appear in the literary magazine *Los cuatro vientos* (The Four Winds). Produces *Amor de don Perlimplín con Belisa en su jardín* (*The Love of Perlimplín with Belisa in the Garden*). *Blood Wedding*, the first play of the "tragic trilogy," is produced. Takes *Blood Wedding*, *Mariana Pineda*, and *The Shoemaker's Prodigious Wife* to Buenos Aires, Argentina, where they enjoy great success. Lectures extensively and also directs one of the plays of seventeenth-century Spanish playwright Lope de Vega.
1934	On the death of the bullfighter and his close friend, writes the poetic elegy "*Llanto por Ignacio Sánchez Mejías*" ("Lamentation for Ignacio Sánchez Mejías"). *Yerma*, the second play of the trilogy, is a triumph in Madrid with Margarita Xirgu in the title role.
1935	*Doña Rosita la soltera o El lenguaje de las flores* (*Rosie the Spinster; or, The Language of Flowers*), with Margarita Xirgu's company, opens in Barcelona. *Christopher's Little Stage* is produced in Madrid. *Seis poemas gallegos* (*Six Galician Poems*) is published.
1936	Publishes *Primeras canciones* (*First Songs*), which he wrote in 1922. Completes his final drama of the trilogy, and the last play he will ever write, *La casa de Bernarda Alba* (*The House of Bernarda Alba*). Leaves Madrid for Granada, where he is one of the earliest casualties of the Spanish civil war. Killed 19 August in Víznar (in the province of Gránada) by Falangist forces.
1937	*Los títeres de cachiporra: Tragicomedia de don Cristóbal y la señá Rosita* (*The Billy Club Puppets: Tragicomedy of*

Christopher and Rosie), written in 1923, is produced in Madrid.

1940   *Poet in New York* is published posthumously in Mexico; *Divan del Tamarit* (*Divan of Tamarit*) is published posthumously in New York.

1945   *The House of Bernarda Alba* has its world premiere in Buenos Aires.

1964   *The House of Bernarda Alba* appears on stage in Madrid.

1975   Lorca's friend Rafael Martínez Nadal publishes an autograph and transcription of *The Audience,* going against Lorca's request when he entrusted Martínez Nadal with the manuscript in 1936.

1978   Under the direction of Miguel Narros, the Teatro Estable Company presents the first professional production in Madrid of *As Five Years Pass. Comedia sin título* (*Untitled Play*) appears in the same volume with the more or less complete text of *The Audience.*

1981   *Lola la comedianta* (*Lola the Prankster*), the libretto of what was supposed to be an opera in one act with music by Manuel de Falla, is published.

1982   The Spanish journal *Títere* publishes the text of Lorca's early one-act play *The Girl Who Waters the Basil and the Inquisitive Prince,* which was thought to be a lost work.

1984   *Sonetos del amor oscuro* (*The Sonnets of Dark Love*) is published in the Spanish newspaper *ABC.*

1989   Miguel Narros presents a new production of *As Five Years Pass* at the Teatro Español in Madrid. The critics find it to be more spectacular but less poetic than the original production. Lluís Pasqual directs the first professional production in Madrid of *Untitled Play* at the Centro Dramático Nacional María Guerrero.

Historical and Literary Context

chapter 1

Lorca's Literary Formation

Federico García Lorca lived his 38 years during one of the most significant periods in both modern Spanish and world history. The dates of his birth (1898) and death (1936) are easy to remember: he was born in the year that Spain went to war with the United States, to which it lost the last colonies of what had once been a great empire. He died in the year that Spain went to war with itself, his life thereby achieving the kind of circular unity that he used in his last play.

Spain is a country with a rich tradition in the theater. It is helpful in understanding Lorca's contribution to Spanish drama to have at least a general idea of two periods in the theatrical history of the country. The Golden Age (roughly the sixteenth and seventeenth centuries) was Spain's greatest moment in the arts. Velázquez, Murillo, and Zurbarán were painting. The Spanish novel began with Fernando de Rojas's creation of *La Celestina,* whose title character remains the prototype of the meddlesome old woman who tries to force love's hand, for a profit. An anonymous author created the picaresque character in *Lazarillo de Tormes,* and Jorge de Montemayor used the Italian model of the pastoral novel in his *Los siete libros de la Diana* (*Seven Books of Diana*). Miguel de Cervantes wrote the masterpiece,

Don Quijote de la Mancha. Luis de Góngora was trying to elevate Spanish poetry to the level of that of classical literature, and Fray Luis de León was looking to Latin poetry as his inspiration for describing the serenity of nature. In the theater, Pedro Calderón de la Barca was giving Spain such philosophical and religious works as *La vida es sueño* (*Life Is a Dream*), and Tirso de Molina created the archetype of the Spanish lover in the character of Don Juan, the protagonist of *El burlador de Sevilla* (*The Seducer of Seville*). But the Spanish stage was dominated by Félix Lope de Vega, to whom as many as 1,800 plays have been attributed, including his masterpiece *Fuenteovejuna* (*Sheep Well*). Lorca directed the three plays mentioned here; his dramatic formation was rooted in Golden Age drama. In addition, Lorca's aesthetic was influenced by traditional European puppet farce.

While Spain had its impressive works of neoclassicism, romanticism, realism, and naturalism during the eighteenth and nineteenth centuries, it is to the situation in the theater during the first quarter of the twentieth century that one must turn to understand the enormity of Lorca's contribution to the stage. As the nineteenth century turned into the twentieth, the Spanish public was watching well-made plays of the realistic, conventional type. Lorca—as well as other members of his artistic generation, for instance, Jacinto Grau and writers of the Generation of 1898, Ramón del Valle-Inclán and Azorín—changed all that. They put poetry (rather than mere verse) on stage and forced the audience's tastes and sensibilities to grow with their daring techniques and often controversial subject matter.

During Lorca's lifetime, the arts were giving birth to new forms that struggled to grow into maturity. It was the period of Dada and surrealism. In Lorca's native Spain, Dalí and Miró, Picasso and Gris, were permanently altering the face of the plastic arts. Buñuel was placing his inimitable stamp on film. Manuel de Falla and Andrés Segovia were weaving popular threads into Spanish classical music. The Generation of 1927 would put Lorca and his circle into the forefront of poetry. In France, Jean Cocteau and Alfred Jarry were writing for the stage, and André Breton and Paul Eluard were liberating poetic form for the twentieth century, as Victor Hugo had liberated it for the nineteenth century. In this century as in the last, the French were to create the literary theories that the Spanish were to bring to fruition in practice. During the period of romanticism, the French broke the bounds of classical drama, but it was the Spanish playwright Duque de Rivas who wrote *Don Alvaro*, the definitive romantic play. So it was in the twentieth century: the French wrote the manifestos, and Lorca wrote *Así que pasen cinco años* (*As Five Years Pass*), which has been hailed as the most accomplished example of surrealistic theater.

Lorca's oeuvre is a reflection of the changes that took place in Western literature during his lifetime, of the cultural milieu in which he lived, and of the artistic influence of his large circle of friends. From his earliest childhood, Lorca wrote little plays for presentation to his family and the servants. He beamed as they applauded his juvenile efforts. He always knew that he wanted to be a writer, to participate in the arts. His one stumbling block was his father, who would not hear of his son's literary aspirations—no son of his was going to be a poet; Federico would study law and be a responsible member of society. Federico's early ambitions may never have been expressed by him more eloquently than in his insect fantasy *El maleficio de la mariposa* (*The Butterfly's Evil Spell*). It is in fact about a sensitive young poet who struggles against the pressures of traditional society in pursuit of poetic perfection and ideal beauty in life. Lorca was putting into practice in his life the hopes of the character that he created: both were going against the tide and taking chances. To a Madrid audience that had been nurtured on the traditional fare of such writers as Jacinto Benavente and the Alvarez Quintero brothers, Lorca introduced a play in which live actors took the parts of insects (roaches, worms, a spider, a butterfly) and all dressed for their parts. Despite an elaborate production, the play barely survived one performance. All but the writer's closest friends walked out in disgust and left the playwright in dismay. It is to Lorca's credit that he could attempt to produce a second play for the stage.

Probably no other detail was so significant in the playwright's life as that of living in Granada, a city rich in history and tradition. Granada, the site of the Moorish palace Alhambra, was the last city that

A scene from the only performance of El maleficio de la mariposa, 22 March 1920.
Courtesy of the Fundación Federico García Lorca.

the Christians were to capture from the Muslims in 1492 in their re-conquest of Arabic Spain. Granada is the home of the gypsies of Spain, as well as of Mariana Pineda, a local heroine in the history of the city and in Lorca's play of the same name. Hers was the first of many great female roles that Federico was to create. Granada was the home of Manuel de Falla, who collaborated with Lorca, and of flamenco music, which found its way into his literature. It provides the setting for *Doña Rosita la soltera* (*Rosie the Spinster*), the idiom for *La zapatera prodigiosa* (*The Shoemaker's Prodigious Wife*), and the folklore for *La Niña que riega la albahaca y el Príncipe preguntón* (The girl who waters the basil and the inquisitive prince).

Lorca lived through two literary generations. The year of his birth gave its name to the Generation of 1898, which included Miguel de Unamuno, José Martínez Ruiz (Azorín), Pío Baroja, Ramón del Valle-Inclán, Antonio Machado, Jacinto Benavente, and Ramiro de Maeztu. Lorca was still a child when they began putting their mark on Spanish literature and did not participate in their examination of Spain's past and present, of what problems in the Spanish land and people caused the country to fall from the international power that it had been in the sixteenth century to the second-rate nation that lost a war to that upstart country across the sea, the United States of America.

Lorca participated in the second Spanish literary movement of the twentieth century, the Generation of 1927. That date marks the three-hundredth anniversary of the death of Luis de Góngora, the most erudite of Spanish poets. Góngora celebrated the metaphor, carrying it to its limits. His poetry was hermetic, closed to many readers of his day and open only to those intellectuals who could understand his cerebral imagery and structure. So too did Lorca's circle pay homage to metaphors and enrich Spanish literature in the process. The group included such immortal names as those of Vicente Aleixandre, Jorge Guillén, Rafael Alberti, Luis Cernuda, and Dámaso Alonso—the last of whom became president of the Royal Spanish Academy of the Language.

Lorca's work is a blend of surrealistic imagery and popular folklore. The gypsies loved his rhythms in *Romancero gitano* (*Gypsy Ballads*); the intellectuals esteemed his daring in the collection *Poeta en Nueva York* (*Poet in New York*). Both elements were to comingle in his theater. His dramatic repertoire is as diverse as it is brief. It includes farces for puppets and for humans, historical drama, surrealism, and poetic tragedy.

Although Lorca was a member óf the Generation of 1927, whose members wrote art for art's sake, Lorca was also a social crusader and used his pen to combat injustice. He attacked the unfair treatment of the gypsies in his native land. In *Gypsy Ballads,* he depicts the often neglected and always persecuted gypsies of Andalusia, where gypsies are accorded the lowest possible social position. Intended to expose the plight of the gypsies, two of the poems in *Gypsy Ballads* are about the fate of a fictional gypsy: "*Prendimiento de Antoñito el Camborio en el camino de Sevilla*" ("The Arrest of Tony Camborio on the Road to Seville") and "*Muerte de Antonio el Camborio*" ("The Death of Anthony Camborio"). In these poems, Lorca depicted an innocent gypsy walking along a road on his way to a bullfight. For no apparent reason, five members of Spain's Civil Guard, which patrols the roads, arrest him and put him in jail. The poems are as much minidramas as Lorca's plays are extended works of poetry.

When Lorca made his trip to New York, he saw similarities between the plight of the blacks in America and that of the gypsies in Spain, and he had to champion their cause, too. Lorca hated New York: he saw it as unemotional, impersonal, and mechanical. What little he did manage to like—New York's only "heart," or rather, "soul"—he found on his long walks alone through Harlem. The blacks won his sympathies and stimulated his creative juices. He saw them as pure and associated them with images from the world of nature. In two of the poems in *Poet in New York,* "*Norma y paraíso de los negros*" ("The Natural State and Paradise of the Blacks") and "*Oda al rey de Harlem*" ("Ode to the King of Harlem"), the author showed through a series of images the contrast between the African soil on which the blacks once lived and the asphalt of Harlem on which they now live. Through this contrast, he was able to depict the anguish of the blacks in their new and unnatural surroundings.

Nowhere was Lorca more passionate in his crusade against injustice than when he wrote about the role of women in Spain. That subject dominated his last four plays, three of which compose the tragic trilogy. The play that is not a part of the trilogy, and the only one of the four that does not end in death, is *Rosie the Spinster.* The three acts of that play trace the life of the title character from the time she enters womanhood until she is well into maturity. It is Rosita's fate in life not to marry and thereby to accept the demeaning role and personal stigma that Spanish society places on spinsterhood. Lorca showed her meaningless life of sitting at home and accepting visits from the most frivolous of friends. (The married women in the play demonstrate maturity; the single women are merely silly girls whose conversation centers on hopes for marriage.) By the end of the play, the housekeeper refers with sympathy to the woman no man will ever want to marry now that she is almost a relic.

The three plays under consideration in this book represent the culmination of all the character types, themes, and techniques that Lorca developed throughout his career. The plays are the result of artistic refinement and maturity. Lorca does not state the specific geographical location of the pieces, but the landscape of rural Andalusia is pervasive. *Bodas de sangre* (*Blood Wedding*) takes place, in part, in a cave inspired by the caves in the Sacromonte area of Granada. *La casa de Bernarda Alba* (*The House of Bernarda Alba*) takes place in a small town of Castille, but the family on which Lorca modeled the characters lived in his area of Granada. Only *Yerma* takes place in a location for which no geographical region is indicated, and there are good reasons for that artistic decision, as a later chapter will reveal.

In all three plays, the principal characters are females (as they are in so many of Lorca's earlier works too), and it is in these works that Lorca showed his deep concern for the needs of women. In these plays, he dealt specifically with the second-class social status ascribed to women in his native land. The three problems that are treated in depth later in this study are a woman's right to marry the man she loves, the social stigma of being a childless woman, and the effects of sexual repression. The plays include poetry, song and dance, and a wealth of customs and beliefs, all of which will be treated in detail in their appropriate chapters.

chapter 2
_____

The Importance of the Works

Blood Wedding, Yerma, and *The House of Bernarda Alba* have won
a place among the great works of world literature in equal measure
for aesthetic and thematic reasons. Since these works are plays intended for presentation on the stage, they have a dimension not found
in the novel, poetry, short story, or essay. In this study, the plays are
considered finished works of literature rather than texts for theatrical
productions.

The main functions of literature are to entertain and to inform.
The plays of the trilogy are gripping in their dramatic tension, engag-
ing in their character development, satisfying in their poetic language,
and stimulating in their transcendent themes. In addition to offering
entertainment, these plays paint a vivid picture of the society that they
portray. More than anything else, they reveal the psychology of the
Spanish people and the values and customs that form the basis of their
society. But if their appeal were solely national rather than universal,
they would not have enjoyed their international success and immense
popularity. While these plays illuminate Spanish attitudes, they also
express universal concerns. *Blood Wedding,* for example, is in part
about a young man who wants his mother to like the woman he is

going to marry, and in part about the mother's concern for her son's welfare. It is also about a woman's desire to be emotionally and physically fulfilled, and about a man who made the mistake of marrying a woman other than the one he truly loved. In another of its aspects, it shows the value of the land as a means of livelihood and as a measure of wealth. In those respects, there is a common denominator between our society and Spanish society that binds rather than separates the nations. Literature points out not only differences but also similarities. It promotes understanding among peoples.

Yerma tells the story of a married woman who is unable to conceive a child. The play takes place in an unidentified society that is somewhere between pagan and mythic, but the anguish of the heroine is the same as that in any nation of the world and at any time in history.

The daughters in *The House of Bernarda Alba* want freedom and men in their lives. How are their needs and desires different from those of young (and not so young) women at any time, in any place? How different would any other daughters act if they were under the control of a tyrannical mother? The play is also about a mother who believes that she is doing what is necessary for her daughters to grow up decently. And who has not been gripped by the fear of gossip that controls the members of this household?

These concerns are not expounded in dry form but are embodied in characters who take on life: they live and breathe and suffer and die. The language of the plays is elegant in its simplicity and grand in its poetry. It took Lorca only a word or two to evoke a location or a mood. For example, the room that is the setting of the first scene of *Blood Wedding* is described as yellow, an unpleasant color in Spanish society. The author leaves it to the mind of the reader (or director) to fill in the details. The conversations consist of a few words per character and thus establish tension. At the other extreme are poetic passages replete with imagery from the natural world—flowers and animals, each with a function in the world. While the plays end in death, they also celebrate life and lament that not every individual is able to participate in the greatness of the surrounding world.

Blood Wedding, Yerma, and *The House of Bernarda Alba* are important plays because they are the most accomplished and mature efforts of the finest Spanish playwright of the twentieth century. Their value is intrinsic as well as transcendental. Lorca remains a great literary figure in part because of the quality of his writing and in equal measure because his works transcend the time and place in which they were written. They are timeless and universal. The implications of his works are far-reaching because the author spoke out not only for gypsies, blacks, and women but for all individuals who cannot accept the role ascribed to them. He gave encouragement to all minorities as well as a warning to society of the consequences of keeping any of its members repressed. Lorca forces his readers to consider the other side of social issues. Why should gypsies be persecuted simply because they are gypsies? Why should blacks be relegated to the position of janitors? Is Romeo's love for Juliet less genuine if both characters are played by men rather than a man and a woman? Should a wife's womanhood be considered diminished because she is not a mother or a husband's manhood called into question because he does not want to be a father?

The plays that compose the trilogy employ a wide range of dramatic techniques. *Blood Wedding* employs such supernatural or surrealistic effects as making the moon a character on stage and having it embody the figure of death. *Yerma* is an intense character study that focuses entirely on the title character. All the action and imagery serve to depict one woman's struggle to overcome a problem over which she has no control. This second play serves as a bridge between the first and the third. Lorca gave some of the mythic symbolism of *Blood Wedding* while making it a modern tragedy. It was Lorca's stated intention in *Yerma* to depict the classical tragedy of the barren woman. *The House of Bernarda Alba* has none of the surrealistic elements of the other two plays and is the author's most mature effort at composing a modern tragedy. In fact, *Blood Wedding* and *Bernarda Alba* are often included in anthologies as examples of surrealistic drama and modern tragedy, respectively.

All three plays are perennial favorites for collegiate productions;

they are presented year after year in country after country because their beauty and meaning never fade. As Lorenzo López Sancho, the drama critic for the Spanish newspaper *ABC*, wrote of the 1989 production of Lorca's *Comedia sin título* (*Untitled Play*), "Lorca continues to be an author rigorously of the moment."[1] What Lorca wrote in the Spain of the 1930s remains important in form and meaning for the world of the 1990s—and beyond.

chapter 3

Critical Reception

The playwright was helpful in identifying the three plays under consideration in this book as a trilogy and on stating his purpose in writing each play. He revealed in an interview in 1934 that he intended to write a trilogy of plays composed of *Blood Wedding, Yerma,* and a play he referred to as both "*La destrucción de Sodoma*" (The destruction of Sodom) and "*El drama des las hijas de Loth*" (The drama of the daughters of Lot). There is no evidence that he ever wrote plays with those titles. In all probability, the second was the working title of the play that finally became *The House of Bernarda Alba*—the play is, after all, about five daughters. He said of *Blood Wedding* that it was a dramatic work that has the effect of hammer blows of poetry from the first scene to the last; that he used poetry to heighten the especially dramatic moments; that for him the most satisfying scene was the one in which the Moon and Death appear on stage in personified form. Lorca called *Blood Wedding* the first part of a dramatic trilogy about the Spanish land. He said that the second play (*Yerma*) would be about the barren woman. He called *Blood Wedding* and *Yerma* "tragedies" rather than mere "dramas." He wanted no plot in the second play—pure and simple tragedy—with a chorus whose function would be to expound on the action of the protagonists. The third play, which turned out to be *The House of Bernarda Alba,* was to depart from the first two in that it would not contain a single drop of poetry. He meant that the play would contain no *verse*: poetry is inherent in the play's conception.

The plays of the trilogy have been produced all over the world, from the time of their writing until the present day. (*The House of Bernarda Alba* could not be produced in Madrid in 1936, at the time of the outbreak of the Spanish civil war, or in the early years of the Franco regime. Its premiere took place in Buenos Aires in 1945. The climate in Madrid would not permit its presentation there until 1964.) It would be impractical, if not impossible, to list all the productions that the plays have received. In general, this review of critical reception limits itself to major, professional productions in Spain (and Argentina in the case of *Bernarda Alba*), as well as the United States and other English-speaking countries. (Criticism of the plays as works of literature will be treated in subsequent chapters.)

Blood Wedding opened in Madrid on 8 March 1933, and its success was immediate and overwhelming. M. Fernández Almagro, writing for the newspaper *El Sol* (The Sun), found that its dramatic elements derived from the poetry of the *Gypsy Ballads* as well as Lorca's earlier plays *The Shoemaker's Prodigious Wife* and *Mariana Pineda*. He mentioned its violent and electrifying atmosphere, its passion, and the effect of its language. He thought that the geographical location was of little consequence and that the importance of the play is in its depiction of human beings whose destinies are controlled by the flaws in their characters. He concluded that this play of "body and soul" reflects a primitive spirit; that it is a "stupendous rural tragedy"; and that "all of it is animated by a sense of the plastic arts, which is the whole secret of and reason for theater."[1]

The reviewer for *ABC* commented on the dialogue, which conveys the rudimentary simplicity of instincts. He found the third act to be inferior to the first two because, in his opinion, the playwright got carried away with poetic symbolism. He compared the characterization to that of Sophocles—motivated by destiny, but withdrawn into the terror of desperation.[2]

In 1935, *Blood Wedding* opened at the Lyceum Theatre in New

York in a production directed by Irene Lewisohn, who was instrumental in bringing it to America. It is obvious from the comments of the reviewers of the original American production that the play lost something in translation. The problem of translation began with the title, which became *Bitter Oleander*. Robert Garland thought that in translation the prose sounded like poetry and the poetry like prose.[3] Brooks Atkinson considered the production so consciously stylized that nothing of the play came across to the audience.[4] Percy Hammond summed up the failure of both the words and images to cross from the Hispanic to the American culture: he called the play "a perfumed package, filled with waxy flowers of speech woven around a semi-tragic tale of passion."[5] Gilbert W. Gabriel thought that the enumeration of floral imagery sounded like a seed catalog rather than a play.[6]

There were some favorable reviews by critics who could see through Jose A. Weissberger's faulty translation. Burns Mantle, for example, realized that the strength of the play lies in its very simplicity. Richard Lockridge found that, translated into a foreign tongue, many of the idiomatic turns of phrase were "often surprising and sometimes comic, but more frequently strangely and freshly effective." He concluded that "at its best the play has poignant beauty."[8]

Dorothy Nichols had no problem with the floral imagery or the cultural milieu. She wrote of a 1952 production at the Actors' Workshop in San Francisco that "once in a long while a play has such an impact that you want to leave the theater without speaking to anyone, without coming out from under its spell." She found *Blood Wedding* to have that impact.[9]

There is no telling what liberties the Art Institute of Chicago took with its production of the play in April 1953. The program lists the cast, in order of appearance, as Death (as the Beggar Woman) and the Moon, appearing on stage before the Mother. There must have been a prologue that foreshadowed the deaths in the third act. In the same year, the Saddler Wells dance company presented *Blood Wedding* as a ballet in London.

In 1958, *Blood Wedding* returned to New York in a production directed by Patricia Newhall at the Actors' Playhouse. The reviews of this production were more favorable than they had been in 1935. The title of the review by John McClain was "Poetic Quality Offers Compelling Evening."[10] Brooks Atkinson found the play to be a work of "terrible beauty," with the grace of the swoop of an eagle.[11]

There were also productions in New York by INTAR in 1980 and by the Repertorio Español in 1984. According to Michiko Kakutani, the INTAR production was more tableau than drama, more surrealistic than conventional narrative.[12] The production at the Repertorio Español was presented in the original Spanish version. The most recent production in this country was presented by the Great Lakes Theater Festival, with direction by Gerald Freedman. It opened at the Ohio Theater in Cleveland on 8 October 1988 and at the Coconut Grove Playhouse in Miami on 9 December 1988. Marianne Evett thought the culture felt alien and yet at the same time as universal as Greek tragedy.[13] Norma Nuirka found the production in Miami to be more a staged poem than a play.[14] The production had music (by John Morris) and dance (choreographed by Graciela Daniela) in addition to the dialogue. The director stated that no one will ever stage a perfect *Blood Wedding* in English because "the music of the language is really impossible to translate; the images have too many connotations."[15] Arnold Mittelman, artistic director of the Coconut Grove Playhouse, insisted that "*Blood Wedding* is not a pageant play or a historical drama, but it has that feeling; it is a family play, for it shows mothers protecting their children."[16] Christine Arnold thought the play was "arresting in its imagery." She praised the striking sets by John Ezell, the paintings by Juan González, the eerie lighting by Perry Eisenhower, and the startling costumes by Jeanne Burton. She admitted that, for someone not steeped in Lorca, the production was emotionally elusive and seldom moving, albeit sometimes fascinating and often commanding. She blamed the loss of the play's poetry on the translation by Michael Dewell and Carmen Zapata, finding it "culturally adrift" in English and lacking the "impassioned rhythms and crescendos and fluid beauty of Spanish."[17]

Blood Wedding was presented in dance by the Ballet Nacional de España (Spanish National Ballet) in December 1988, with direction and choreography by Antonio Gades. In 1981, Gades also choreographed an effective film version in flamenco dance and interpreted the role of the Bridegroom (*Novio*). Alfredo de Mañas provided the adaptation to dance, Emilio de Diego composed the score, and Carlos Saura directed. It is available on videocassette.

Yerma has had less success in the United States than *Blood Wedding* and *The House of Bernarda Alba*. One reason might be that it has neither the spectacular, surrealistic effects of the former nor the classical lines of the latter. A second reason might be that it is the most difficult of the three to translate adequately; both the imagery and the psychology are alien to audiences outside of the Hispanic world. A society preoccupied with birth control and abortion may find it difficult to accept the turmoil of a woman who is unable to conceive a child. It is a pity that *Yerma* is a bit neglected, since it is Lorca's most beautiful work, perhaps the most beautiful in all of Spanish drama.

Lorca stated in a 1934 interview that he intended to write the tragedy of the barren woman as a work along classical lines with four principal characters and choruses (1759–60).[18] The play opened at the Teatro Español in Madrid on 29 December 1934 to overwhelming success. In fact, E. Díez-Canedo entitled his review of the opening "*Yerma*, Federico García Lorca's Tragic Poem, Had Extraordinary Success at the Español Theater." He went on to state that there no longer existed any doubt that Lorca was now as accomplished a playwright as a poet.[19] The reviewer for *ABC* wrote of its poetic vision of the drama of life and stated that in fact the play is a dramatized poem, more the work of a poet than of a playwright.[20] Luis Araujo Costa criticized *Yerma* for not really being theater, citing its lack of dramatic action.[21] On the other hand, Alejandro Miquis (whose review refers to "García Llorca"!) found the play to be a veritable modern tragedy with the classical stamp of fatality and an abundance of pictorial energy. He called it an admirable theatrical work.[22] For Alberto Marín Alcalde, the opening was a "definitive triumph. . . . Everything that occurs in the work is the internal process of the spirit of woman." He also identified the Washerwomen as serving the function of a Greek chorus.[23] Lino Novás Calvo contrasted Lorca with his contemporaries: only Lorca was doing something good for the theater; he called *Yerma* a magnificent work with a transcendental theme and sustained dramatic realization.[24] A 1937 review that appeared in Buenos Aires reported that the play is about a woman fighting against her destiny; the force of truth in the play left the spectators overcome with emotion. The reviewer found the language to be lively and the playwright sincere.[25]

Yerma appeared in New York in 1947 with Bea Arthur in the title role. The *New York Morning Telegraph*'s review of the off-Broadway production at the Cherry Lane Theater in Greenwich Village was titled "On-Stage's Best Play of Season."[26] Another bit of interesting casting took place in the Terzo Festival dei Due Mondi at the Teatro Nuovo in Spoleto, Italy, in July 1960. Concha García Lorca, the playwright's sister, played the part of the Old Woman (*Vieja*) in the production directed by Luis Escobar. When the Repertory Theater of Lincoln Center in New York presented *Yerma* at the Vivian Beaumont Theater, Frank Langella had the role of Juan. Whitney Bolton believed that the play lost something of its beauty in English translation. He stated that "the difference between Lorca in his own language and that given to us in translation is the difference between the sparkle of spring water and the bleak of autumn."[27] In sharp contrast the Bolton, Edward Sothern Hipp thought that the direction of John Hirsch, from Canada's Stratford Festival, made the brooding, sprawling folk tragedy work beautifully.[28] And while the title of the review in the *New York World Journal Tribune* was "*Yerma* too Un-Spanish,"[29] the review in the *Village Voice* called the play inaccessible to American audiences for its narrowly Spanish themes and sensibilities, saturated with "petrified, repressive moral codes, and almost lascivious fatalism, a darkly beautiful sense of impending doom."[30]

The 1972 production of *Yerma* in Spanish by the Nuria Espert Company at the Brooklyn Academy of Music attracted a great deal of critical attention; it was directed by Víctor García, with Espert playing Yerma. Edith Oliver observed that the play is entirely concerned with fertility, and she noted the contrasting imagery of aridity versus fecundity and wetness. She said that Yerma's dryness accounts for the fact that she never sheds a tear during her grief. Much of Oliver's review focused on the production—the stylized acting and choreographed movement, the trampoline for a stage and the two nude characters during the fertility rite. She concluded that "even in translation the lines are still poetry," and that the production was "an experience [she] won't forget."[31]

Her sentiments were echoed by Michael Feingold writing in the *Village Voice*. He found part of the beauty to be the Spanish, which was no problem for the spectator who did not understand the language. For him the trampoline suggested the mean, arbitrary cosmos that destroys Yerma's happiness.[32] For Henry Hewes, the trampoline was a womblike canvas that was constantly changing its function—floor, wall, ceiling, sky, hill, and plain. He found it to be a living organism against which the actors could act and react.[33] The reviewer for the *New Leader* found the Espert Company to be reminiscent of Jerzy Grotowski and Peter Brook's system of freehandedly reinterpreting the classics.[34] Martin Gottfried found the set to be the star of the show.[35]

Yerma was presented at the Stratford (Canada) Season in 1979 in a freely adapted version by Pam Brighton and the company. There was an attempt to produce a musical version of *Yerma* in 1958; but the production was unsuccessful in its tryouts at the University of Denver and Ithaca College, and it never reached Broadway. The translation into English was by Paul Bowles, who also composed the score.

The House of Bernarda Alba had its debut in Buenos Aires (a city that Lorca had visited in 1933) on 8 March 1945 at the Avenida Theater. Margarita Xirgu played the title character, in accordance with Lorca's wishes. Samuel Eichelbaum's review, "Federico García Lorca's Posthumous Play," identified the influence of Lope de Vega on Lorca's scenic poetry. He saw the suffering in the characters' spirits as well as the playwright's presence by means of the note at the beginning of the text.[36] An unsigned review in *La Nación* (The Nation) identified Lorca's work with that of Calderón de la Barca, in both of which honor is at the core of the plays. In this play—about the obsession with virginity and the tragic destiny in life—the playwright as strong realist dominates over the poet.[37]

Another unsigned review, this one in *Blanco y negro* (White and Black), traced the pattern in the trilogy. It called *Blood Wedding* the nuptial tragedy, *Yerma* the tragedy of frustrated motherhood, and *The House of Bernarda Alba* the tragedy of virginity. The reviewer found that *Bernarda Alba* "implicitly completes the trilogy of profound elemental roots and high lyrical flight." In addition, "the tragic inspiration of García Lorca reaches its summit in this work."[38]

Despite Lorca's specific directions for the changes in the scenic design in the play's three acts (discussed in detail in Chapter 7), the program for the production at the Crescent Theatre in Birmingham, England, in 1952 states that both acts 1 and 2 take place in a white room in the home of Bernarda Alba during the summer. The play also ran for 17 performances at the ANTA Theater in New York in January 1951.

Four years before the play reached the Madrid stage, it was presented on American television in the "Play of the Week" series. Anne Revere played the title role, Eileen Heckart was the housekeeper, La Poncia; and Suzanne Pleshette played Adela. John P. Shanley, reviewing the television production in the *New York Times,* compared the grief and anguish of this play with similar aspects of the later works of Tennessee Williams.[39]

A year before the opening in Madrid, Lee Brewer directed the Actors' Workshop in the play at the Encore Theater in San Francisco. The play was a resounding success. According to Stanley Eichelbaum, it was "superbly atmospheric to the eye and gloriously affecting to the ear."[40] Because *Bernarda Alba* was written in prose rather than verse and deals with the subject of personal freedom, it is more successful in English translation than *Yerma.* The absence of floral images also makes it more accessible than *Blood Wedding* to American audiences.

The House of Bernarda Alba opened at the Goya Theater in Madrid on 10 January 1964. It was presented by Martiza Caballero's company and directed by Juan Antonio Bardem. Antonio Saura, the brother of film director Carlos Saura and now a renowned artist, designed the sets. Enrique Llovet reviewed the production for *ABC.* As reviewers had done before him, Llovet also identified Lopesque and Calderonian elements in Lorca. He saw in the play the range of Spanish characteristics—envy, resentment, resignation, and honor—and concluded that it is indeed a rigorously modern tragedy, "very probably one of the greatest works in Spanish dramatic literature of the twentieth century."[41]

There were three Spanish-language productions of *Bernarda Alba* in New York during the 1970s, and apparently there was no language barrier for English-speaking audiences. Howard Thompson recommended the 1972 production at the ADAL Theater even for those who could not understand Spanish.[42] *Show Business* found the 1974 production of *Bernarda Alba* at Nuestro Teatro (Our Theater) to be "Lorca at Its Best"; it "can be appreciated even by those unfamiliar with the Spanish language. Nuestro Teatro glorifies once again the universal language of drama."[43] Finally, in 1979, the Repertorio Español had a production that captured the "somber strength of the writing."[44] The Repertorio Español produced the work again in 1989, and the unnamed author of a short review in the *New Yorker* stated how vital rather than dated the play had remained. Apparently, teenage girls at one production strongly identified with the claustrophic lives led by the women of the play, and with the play's refrain "¡Déjame salir!" (Let me go!)[45] There have also been college productions from Berkeley to Yale and from South Dakota to Howard University, as well as by the University of Cape Town (South Africa) Dramatic Society.

The British were treated to Lorca's work during the 1980s. In 1985, the Oxford Playhouse hosted the Nuria Espert production of *Yerma,* and a year later the Edinburgh Festival presented *Blood Wedding.* Also in 1986, the Lyric Theatre in Hammersmith, England, produced *The House of Bernarda Alba,* directed by Nuria Espert, with Glenda Jackson as Bernarda and Joan Plowright as La Poncia. After a sell-out run at the Lyric, the production moved with great success to the Globe Theatre on the West End.

Lorca had great success as a playwright during his lifetime, and his reputation has grown steadily since his death. In part because of his trilogy, in part because of his poetry (especially the *Gypsy Ballads* and "*Llanto por Ignacio Sánchez Mejías*"["Lamentation for Ignacio

Sánchez Mejías"]), and in part because of the sensational circumstances of his death, he has taken on larger-than-life proportions. The bibliography on Lorca is abundant and continues to proliferate. In recent years, scholarship on Lorca has even surpassed that of such towering figures as Lope de Vega and Miguel de Cervantes. A large portion of the writing on Lorca's plays deals with the trilogy, with more work on *The House of Bernarda Alba* than on any other single work. Studies of just the three plays account for more than half the work on his theater.

Unfortunately, the scholarship is qualitatively uneven. There are many fine studies listed in the bibliography of this book; most of them are by dedicated Hispanists who are qualified to write on his work because they have carefully studied the original texts. Other works, generally occasional pieces or biographical notes, are by individuals in his enormous circle of friends; the feelings raised by the circumstances of his death have produced much work of an emotional, sentimental, and even frivolous nature. Another body of scholarship that often fails to hit the mark is written by non-Hispanists who read Lorca in faulty translation (admittedly, he is not easily translated) and in turn produce studies as imprecise as the translations themselves. What is lacking in translation are the beauty of the imagery and the richness of the language. Since those writers' knowledge of Spanish is often minimal or nonexistent, they cannot avail themselves of the original versions of the plays or of the critical material in Spanish. This is especially true of the three tragedies, which have been the most unfortunate victims of critics who depend upon reading the plays solely in translation. It often appears that they are familiar with neither the rest of Lorca's body of work nor the already existing scholarship. Some Hispanists are equally guilty of duplicating what has already been written, seemingly because they have not read previous studies.

To state that every article by a Hispanist is reliable and that everything written by a non-Hispanist is faulty, however, would be neither true nor fair. A large body of criticism, some of it good, some of it bad, approaches the plays from every possible point of view. Yet another group of critics finds it necessary to attempt to interpret Lorca's work through intimate details of his personal life. They seem to forget that it is his work that remains alive and is an end in itself, and that his private life is just that, private, and should not be subject matter for speculation. Only by approaching Lorca's plays as the product of both a poet and a playwright and by seeing each play as a part of the whole body of his poetry and theater is it possible to do justice to the man who may well have been the most talented author ever to write for the Spanish stage.

A Reading

chapter 4

Structure

There is no problem of becoming overburdened with the details of the plots of the plays of Lorca's trilogy, since they have little or no plot line. He designed his plays to be skeletal so that he could concentrate on other theatrical elements. Despite Lorca's stated purpose of following the Aristotelian canon, he departed immediately from the rules of the Greek master by eliminating the details of telling a story. In *Blood Wedding*, Lorca was concerned with the aspect of "total" theater: drama, music, dance, mise-en-scène. He showed how heavily influenced he was by the stage symbolism of the time in his use of allegorical characters, the Moon and the Beggar Woman, who represent Death. In *Yerma*, Lorca presented a poetic character study of a barren woman. In *The House of Bernarda Alba*, he was presenting a theme embodied in staging that was intended to resemble a photographic document. Of the three plays, only *Blood Wedding* has any plot line at all, and it can be summed up simply: despite his mother's warnings, the Bridegroom (*Novio*) marries the Bride (*Novia*); on the very night of their nuptials, she runs off with Leonardo before the marriage is even consummated; Leonardo and the Bridegroom kill each other in a duel, and the Bride moves in with her mother-in-law. *Yerma* has no plot line at all, except for the passing of time. *Bernarda Alba* is an episodic play.

Lorca subtitled *Blood Wedding* a "Tragedy in Three Acts and Seven Scenes."[1] He used the first act to present the characters and the themes. It makes for interesting, dramatic speculation to try to determine exactly how much time passes in the course of the play. The first scene (*cuadro*)[2] takes place in the morning in the home of the Bridegroom and his widowed mother (*Madre*). The son is ready to leave for his workday in the vineyard, without expecting to get his mother started on lamenting once again the tragedies she has suffered in life—the death of her husband and a son by a knife at the hand of the Félix family—when he asks for his own knife. Within moments of the curtain's rising, Lorca has presented two of the principal characters, their conflict, the Mother's ordeal, the theme of death, the name of the Félix clan, and the images of knives and blood. The abruptness of the opening lines of the .play establishes the tension and closely parallels the opening lines of dialogue in the next play, *Yerma*:

NOVIO:	(Entrando.) *Madre.*
MADRE:	*¿Qué?*
NOVIO:	*Me voy.*
MADRE:	*¿Adónde?*
NOVIO:	*A la viña.* (Va a salir.)
MADRE:	*Espera.* (1171–72)

(BRIDEGROOM:	[*Entering.*] Mother.
MOTHER:	What?
BRIDEGROOM:	I'm going.
MOTHER:	Where?
BRIDEGROOM:	To the vineyard. [*Begins to leave.*]
MOTHER:	Wait.)

Before the scene ends, the Neighbor (*Vecina*) stops for a visit. The Mother, trying to learn what she can of the past of the woman to whom her son is about to be married, discovers that she was once engaged to Leonardo, a member of the Félix family.

The second scene also takes place in the morning. There is no statement that it is the same morning as in the first scene, but it makes good dramatic sense for it to be so: the playwright can thus present concurrent moments in the lives of his various characters. This scene introduces Leonardo, the man to whom the Bride would really like to be married, and his family—a wife (*Mujer*), their baby, and his mother-in-law (*Suegra*).[3] In the lullaby that the Mother-in-Law is singing to put the baby to sleep, two other key images of the play emerge, namely, horses and water. The Wife conversationally breaks the news to Leonardo that tomorrow the Bridegroom will ask for her (the Wife's) cousin's hand in marriage. Leonardo becomes upset and momentarily abusive toward his wife. Just as the Neighbor enters the Bridegroom's house to serve as an outside voice—a messenger—to bring information, so the Girl (*Muchacha*) enters to tell the Mother-in-Law that the Bridegroom has been to the store and bought the best of everything for his intended. She also introduces the first note of sensuality in the play when she points to that part of the Bride's stockings that has a rose—on the thigh—that is not a simple rose but one with a stem and seeds. And here is introduced the subject of money: not only are a man and a woman to be united, but two fortunes. The theme of money is one of the unifying devices in the trilogy. The tears shed by the Wife, the Mother-in-Law, and the Girl are a foreshadowing of the tragedy yet to come.

The third scene takes place on the day following the second scene, and thereby Lorca again departed from the dicta of the Greek theoretician whose model he claimed to wish to follow. Not only is there a change of place from scene to scene, but there is no unity of time—the play does not take place in a single day. It is impossible to determine exactly how much time passes in this play. Only in *Yerma*, in which the passing of time is one of the play's themes, is it possible to do so. The time factor in *Bernarda Alba* is more poetic than it is realistic.

The Mother and the Bridegroom are at the home of the Father

(*Padre*) of the Bride to settle the details of the wedding. The Mother and the Father take the opportunity to extol the virtues and virtue of their children and to discuss the financial arrangements of the marriage. Once again the scene ends with a character from outside of the family acting as a catalyst in identifying another character's problem. This time it is the Maid (*Criada*) of the Bride. Her mere mention of wanting to see the wedding presents that the Bridegroom and the Mother have brought throws the Bride into a rage and thus cracks the calm surface to reveal the strife within her. The third scene of the act takes place during an afternoon; the Bridegroom and the Mother have traveled for four hours to get to the home of the Bride and arrive in the heat of the day. The rest of the play takes place at night. The acts form a single dramatic day, despite the amount of time that transpires between scenes and between acts: there is one morning, one afternoon, and one night.

The second act begins where the first act ended, in the Bride's home. It is the evening of the following Thursday, the date on which the marriage is to take place. Lorca did not state when the scene takes place, but he did leave clues. The reader must keep in mind all the evidence that Lorca presented in the first act to understand the time frame of the second. Not only is there no change of place between the two acts, there is also no change in the characters on stage. This scene begins where the other left off—the Bride is with her maid, who is grooming her for the wedding. Neither the Bride's mood nor the Maid's inquisitiveness has changed. As a matter of fact, during the intervening days both have intensified. It is the moment of truth: tonight the wedding is to take place.

It is perfectly natural for a bride to be nervous on her wedding day, but the Bride is more than nervous: she is on edge, and any mention of the wedding upsets her. Lorca aptly established her uneasiness and then went a step further. He had Leonardo arrive as the first guest at the wedding. The Maid never leaves the former lovers alone; she witnesses their conversation and changes it when the need arises. When the time comes, she grabs Leonardo by the lapel and forces him to leave.

Lorca's plays are structured as dramatic crescendos with a key event around which the rest of the action revolves. Nowhere is that technique more evident than in the second scene of the second act of *Blood Wedding*. In contrast to the previous scene, which took place inside the cave, this one takes place in the open air outside of the cave. The Maid is still in a festive mood and sings as she prepares the table; she is alone onstage as the guests begin to return for the reception after the marriage ceremony in church. If the Bride was irritable before the ceremony, she is now unable to keep a civil tongue with either her bridegroom or her mother-in-law. In the midst of the festivities, Leonardo disappears. The Bride claims to have much to think about and a headache and excuses herself from her husband. It is not long before she too has disappeared. Leonardo's wife announces that the two of them have taken off together. The Mother sends her son after them.

The third act depicts the consequences of the characters' actions in the first two. It is still nighttime, presumably the same night on which act 2 ended. It takes place in a stylized woods whose atmosphere is suggested by tree trunks and the eerie strains of violins. The characters who dominate the first scene of the act are as stylized and symbolic as the setting. Only the Bridegroom—and the Bride and Leonardo, who appear late in the scene—are familiar. (The other characters—the Woodcutters [*Leñadores*], the Moon [*Luna*], and the Beggar Woman [*Mendiga*]—will be treated in Chapter 7). Of the three characters who appear in the first two acts, the Bridegroom is the first to present himself onstage in act 3. He is searching for his wife and her lover but meets instead the Beggar Woman, the physical representation of death. She leads him offstage, clearing it for the second appearance of the Woodcutters, who appeared at the beginning of the scene. They exit as the Bride and Leonardo enter, speaking only in verse in this most poetic of scenes. As the scene closes, Leonardo speaks to the Bride with unconscious irony and yet prophetically about his death. Both vow that only death can part them. The final stage direction indicates two screams, followed by the appearance onstage of the Beggar Woman, who remains center stage with her shawl open to give the appearance of a large bird with immense wings.

The second scene of the act is also the last of the play. As such, it is the dramatic culmination of the tragedy. There is no time indicated for the scene, which takes place in a simple white room that gives the feeling of a church. The scene opens with the poems, songs, and games of the Girls, who are singing of weddings and death through their references to a knife and the color crimson. Their song is interrupted by the entrance of Leonardo's wife and mother-in-law, who also speak in verse. The Girls want to hear all about the wedding, as does the Wife. All the Mother-in-Law can summon herself to tell the Wife is that she should get home, grow old, and cry. The Beggar Woman reappears and announces that she saw the two lovers dead in the night.

With her exit and that of the Girls, Lorca reverted to the prose that he used in the first two acts, before symbolic figures appeared as characters in the play. The unlikely grouping of characters for this, the penultimate segment of the play, is composed of the Mother, the Neighbor from the first act, and the Bride. The Mother is enraged at the Neighbor for her incessant crying; she wants to live out what remains of her life in solitude now that everyone she ever cared for— her husband and both of her sons—is dead. Nor has she any interest in hearing the Bride's explanation for running off with Leonardo, or her assertion that her virtue remains intact. For the final segment of the play, Lorca again used verse, as the Women try to console with religion the Mother, the Wife, and the Bride, who have to confront the reality of the dead bodies of the two men who killed each other for love.

The structure of *Yerma,* a "Tragic Poem in Three Acts and Six Scenes," roughly parallels that of *Blood Wedding.* Lorca was in the process of streamlining his work, and therefore there is far less of a plot in this play than in the last. His concern for Yerma was not only to create a character, but to embody her problem in poetry. There are two time frames at work in this play, the real and the poetic. In the realm of real time, many years pass in the play; in the realm of poetic time, there is one morning, one afternoon, and one night: a poetic day.

What story there is in the play occurs in the opening moments. As the curtain rises on the first scene, Yerma has dozed off with her sewing basket at her feet. Lorca used special lighting effects to indicate that what is happening onstage is a representation of Yerma's dreams. In it, a shepherd enters the stage and stares at Yerma. He is holding by the hand a little child dressed in white. The morning light accompanies the sound of a clock, and Yerma wakes up. She hears a distant voice singing a lullaby. She calls to her husband as he starts to leave for work in the fields. That is the entire play in miniature: Yerma gets the attention of a shepherd, who brings a child to her; when she returns to the world of reality, she is the wife of a man who is always on his way to work. The changes in and structure of the first moments of the play demonstrate stark contrasts: dream versus reality, attention versus avoidance, poetry versus prose, song versus silence, child versus barrenness. When husband and wife speak to each other, their words are few, echoes of the same phrases repeated daily over the two years of their married life:

YERMA: *Juan, ¿me oyes?, Juan.*

JUAN: *Voy.*

YERMA: *Ya es la hora.*

JUAN: *¿Pasaron las yuntas?*

YERMA: *Ya pasaron.*

JUAN: *Hasta luego.* (Va a salir.) (1274)

YERMA: Juan, do you hear me, Juan?

JUAN: I'm coming.

YERMA: It's time.

JUAN: Have the cattle passed?

YERMA: They've already passed.

JUAN: So long. [*Begins to leave.*]

So ends what might be called the opening segment of the play. In fact, the rest of the play is an explanation and elaboration of that fragment.

Yerma stops Juan from leaving; what was abrupt efficiency turns to tension, but in the next few moments Lorca demonstrated the dichotomy in the needs and values of the two characters. Yerma wants to nurture Juan; he wants to be left alone. Yerma wants to have a child; Juan is glad that they do not have any children who cost money. The similarities between the opening of *Yerma* and *Blood Wedding* are striking. Each begins with a dialogue of few words centered on the man leaving for work and then proceeds immediately to the problem that consumes the woman. In *Blood Wedding,* it is the absence of the Mother's dead husband and son; in *Yerma,* it is the absence of a child in the family. Just as the Bridegroom managed to end the conversation by leaving for the fields, so does Juan. With her husband gone, Yerma is left in an empty house and alone with her thoughts. She passes her hand over her barren belly, begins her sewing, and sings to her yet unconceived child. The poem that she recites is the second of a series of songs that in and of themselves tell the story of the play. The first is a lullaby off in the distance to a child Yerma cannot see. The second is the expression of her need for a child in her life. It is also a hymn to nature, a recitation of the function of the fecund world, of which she is not a part. She has been married for 24 months and is still not pregnant.

Just as the Neighbor entered after the son left for work in *Blood Wedding,* so enters María after Juan has left for the fields. María is on her way home from the store, where she has purchased everything that she is going to need for the new arrival in her home: she is pregnant, and after just five months of marriage. Yerma is painfully aware of the fact that she and Juan have been married for two years and twenty days—Yerma keeps track of the passing of time. Did twenty days pass between the opening scene in which Juan goes off to work and the following one with the arrival of María, or is Yerma just more precise around her neighbor than with her husband? Maybe she is not afraid to reveal to María just how carefully she keeps track of the cause of her anguish. Yerma is curious to know every detail of how it feels to be pregnant.

The next segment of the play is the most significant of the first scene, perhaps of the entire play. It is Yerma's chance meeting with Víctor. One has to wonder if the scene is really taking place. As María leaves, Yerma assumes the same position that she was in at the opening of the play. As she removes the scissors from her sewing basket, Víctor appears and asks for Juan. Since Yerma is making diapers (presumably for María's baby), Víctor thinks that Yerma is pregnant; his words almost make her choke. He hardly needs to remind her that there is a definite lack of children in her home. The mere presence of Víctor makes Yerma think of how she is waiting for her baby to arrive—not in the world, but at least in her womb. She breathes deeply the air that Víctor had breathed and then resumes her sewing. The first scene ends where it began, with a perfectly circular structure.

In the second scene of act 1, it is midday and Yerma is returning from having brought lunch to her husband in the fields. On this particular afternoon Yerma has several encounters, the first of which is with *Vieja* 1ª (First Old Woman). Oddly enough, the Old Woman asks how long Yerma has been married. It is now three years. Next she wants to know if Yerma has children. This question, of course, opens the floodgates. First Yerma simply answers no; when the Old Woman assures her that she will be, Yerma's anxiety returns. The Old Woman had fourteen children—five died and nine survived, all males. Yerma has just one question to ask her, but the Old Woman, anticipating what it will be, refuses in advance to answer it: one does not discuss such matters. Yerma will not be put off and wants to know why she is "dry." The Old Woman has her ideas on the subject but refuses to voice them. Yerma now has her first insight into the root of her problem. She and Juan are doing everything they need to physically in order to have a child but are not doing anything emotionally. In Yerma's world, it is not the sexual act alone that brings on pregnancy; the act must take place with both partners in the proper frame of mind. (There will be more on this subject in Chapter 6.)

As the Old Woman leaves, two girls appear (*Muchacha* 1ª and *Muchacha* 2ª) (again, subjects for a later chapter). The first Girl makes the mistake of telling Yerma that she left her child sleeping alone at home, and Yerma is quick to list all the calamities that can befall him. The Second Girl assures Yerma that if she had four or five children of her own, she would no longer be so cautious. Yerma does not think that she would be any different even if she had forty children. The

Second Girl, whose way of thinking is closer to Juan's than to Yerma's, finds life peaceful without children. She mentions that her mother gives her all kinds of potions to take to enhance her fertility, and that in October they are going to visit a holy person who can make her fertile. Before the Girl rushes off, Yerma makes sure that she knows where the Girl's mother lives and what her name is—Dolores—then files the information away in her mind for future reference.

As the Second Girl leaves, Yerma hears Víctor's voice singing. His song and Yerma's song in response turn into a duet, worthy of opera. The songs are replete with suggestions that Víctor would be better off living with her than alone. In Víctor's presence, Yerma thinks that she hears a baby crying, as if submerged somewhere. What she "hears" is the child that she believes she would have had if she had married Víctor. They stare at each other until Víctor, fearfully, averts his eyes. At that moment, Juan arrives and sees Yerma and Víctor together. Juan is furious that his wife is speaking publicly to another man. She will give the neighbors ammunition for gossip about them. He sends his wife home to sleep; he will spend the night irrigating the land.

The first scene of act 2 of *Yerma* is the most beautiful of the trilogy. Some of the imagery of this most poetic scene will be examined in a subsequent chapter, but much of the scene fits into a study of the play's structure. Lorca's stated intention was to write a play along the lines of a Greek tragedy with a chorus commenting on the action. In this scene, the chorus, composed of six washerwomen (*Lavanderas*) washing clothes in the local stream, is the main collective character: it is a social occasion for the women of the town, who have little other opportunity to meet and talk. Despite their claim of not liking to spread gossip, this is the occasion that the women have, away from their husbands, to speak freely. The scene is the physical representation of the gossip that dominates the lives of the characters, Juan in particular (and even more so the household of Bernarda Alba in that play). Much of the text is in verse. The Washerwomen are arranged on various levels on the stage as they sing their song.

Their subject of conversation is Yerma's honor (a subject treated in detail in Chapter 6). The women show little pity for Yerma's plight.

Their attitudes, in fact, indicate not the slightest hint of sympathy for another woman who is suffering for reasons out of her control. They insist that women who want honor have to earn it; that Yerma has so trampled upon the good name of the family that Juan has had his two spinster sisters move in with him to keep an eye on his wife's behavior (thus alerting the reader to the two new characters who will appear in the next scene); and that women who want to have children, do. The women are the voice of the town, the voice of society, the voice of nature, into none of which Yerma is able to fit. If the scene of the Washerwomen is a paean to nature (as a later and detailed examination of the imagery will reveal), the refrain is "¡*Ay de la casada seca! / ¡Ay de la que tiene los pechos de arena!*" (1307; Woe to the married woman who is dry! / Woe to her who has breasts of sand!).

It is late afternoon when the second scene of act 2 takes place in Yerma's home. She is not present when the scene begins, and Juan is berating his sisters for having allowed her to leave the house. As he sees it, their function in his home—in life—is to see that Yerma do nothing to blemish his honor; it is for that reason that he is allowing them to eat from his table and to drink his wine. One reason Juan is so happy that he has no children is that if he did they too would be eating his hard-earned food. He reminds his sisters that his honor is also theirs: they do not have husbands from whom their honor can derive.

It is only a moment later when Yerma returns; she has been to the public fountain to fetch water for dinner. Yerma attempts to speak to her husband about his business, but he is abrupt; he has other things on his mind to discuss with his wife. She has offended his sense of tradition and propriety. Men belong in the fields and women in the home. He is forced to be on the alert at every moment to be certain that Yerma is not doing anything to tarnish his reputation or even give the appearance of doing something that might tarnish his reputation. Sin, after all, is in the mind of the beholder, and the previous scene shows just how ready people are to pass judgment on others. Yerma insists that just as men have their lives, so do women—all except her. Juan can see the subject that Yerma is broaching, and he does not want to hear about it again. He has heard little else during what has now been more than five years of married life. He has come to realize how much Yerma needs to raise a child and offers to let her have one of her nephews move in with them, but that solution is not good enough for Yerma. She needs more than to feed and clothe a child; she needs the entire physiological and emotional experience of producing that child from her own blood. When Juan has finished his diatribe against his wife, he leaves. Yerma, as if in a dream, recites a touching poem on how desperately she needs to have a child she can suffer as he sucks the milk from her bosom and turns them from blind breasts into white doves, which will free her blood from being the prisoner of the wasps that inhabit it.

She ends her song as she notices María, with a child in her arms, hurrying past her door. María has taken to not stopping by when she has a child with her so that she will not make Yerma cry; she hates the envy that she is able to instill in her neighbor. Yerma again tries to explain what it is like for a woman to be childless. María turns the conversation to Juan and his sisters. For Yerma, it is a situation of three against one, a sort of living death. When María's child, whom Yerma has been holding, wakes up, Yerma looks at him and begins to cry. She gently pushes María toward the door. As María leaves, the Second Girl tells Yerma that her mother is waiting for her along with two neighbors. Yerma has no fear of attending the ritual to which the other women are also going.

All of a sudden Víctor appears. This is his third and final appearance in the play: it is the last time Yerma will ever see him. Following his elderly father's advice, he is moving with his two brothers to another location, but he did not want to leave without saying good-bye to Juan. Yerma lets Víctor know that she has never forgotten the one occasion, long ago, when he took her in his arms. What she felt with him at that moment can never change. Unbeknownst to Yerma, Juan has purchased Víctor's flock of sheep. He is prospering economically while his wife withers emotionally. Víctor gives Yerma his hand and wishes her peace for her home. She stares at the hand that Víctor has touched, grabs her wrap, and takes the opportunity to flee to meet

Dolores, while her husband accompanies Víctor as far as the arroyo. The two sisters-in-law call after Yerma as the scene ends in total darkness.

In the third act, Lorca brought to fruition all the seeds that he planted in the first two acts, and the play comes to a rapid climax. In the first scene, at dawn, Yerma is in the house of Dolores the conjurer, who praises Yerma for her courage. Yerma had shown no fear in the cemetery at night when Dolores performed the ritual that was to make Yerma fertile. Yerma is a desperate woman and willing to try anything in her attempts to conceive a child. Dolores assures her that now she will conceive. Despite Dolores's insistence that Juan too wants children, Yerma knows the truth and laments the fact that she needs his participation in the process and cannot produce children alone. It is almost daybreak, the point at which the play began.

Voices are heard outside of the house. They belong to Juan and his two sisters, who have followed Yerma. This is a new affront to Juan's honor, finding his wife in the home of a witch; he can take no more of Yerma's antics, which he has put up with since their wedding day. As Bernarda Alba will in the next play, Juan demands silence.

It is the dark of night in the last scene of the play, which takes place at a hermitage high in the mountains. The stage is filled with barefooted women making offerings. With all else having failed, Yerma takes a potion to make her conceive. Yerma joins in the chorus of women singing a hymn to fertility. Suddenly two figures appear with great masks. One represents male and the other female; they are the very faces of nature. They engage in an erotic song and dance in which the Male (*Macho*) has a horn, full of phallic significance, which he shakes at the Female (*Hembra*). In the midst of the excitement, the Old Woman approaches Yerma with the answer to her question from act 1 and the solution to Yerma's problem. Her barrenness is the fault of Juan, who is of weak seed, unlike Yerma's, which is strong. At the pagan rite, there are more men than women, all eager to impregnate the married women who have not been able to have children with their husbands. The Old Woman's son is one of the men only too eager to offer his services. The Old Woman wants Yerma to leave Juan and come to live with her son and her, thus becoming a mother herself. The very suggestion is repulsive to Yerma's sense of honor. Juan appears at what is the final affront to what is left of his honor and reputation, the presence of his wife at a fertility rite that amounts to little more than a sexual orgy. For the last time, he confronts his wife, then tries to embrace her and be affectionate, to make her understand that he wants her for herself and not as a means to any other end. When he asks her to kiss him, instead she strangles him. With her own hands, Yerma murders her husband and kills any hope that she might one day become a mother. There is a progression in the trilogy from the concept of "total theater," with story line and spectacle, in *Blood Wedding,* to a poetic character study without plot line in *Yerma,* to the "pure theater" of *The House of Bernarda Alba,* which has no real plot or elaborate staging, just the dramatic representation of a theme.[4]

Â Â Â *Bernarda Alba* is the most subtle and classical in structure of the three plays. *Blood Wedding* has symbolic characters representing the Moon and Death. *Yerma* has the erotic dance of the Male and the Female during the fertility rite. *Bernarda Alba* has no such techniques. In *Blood Wedding,* it is necessary to have scenes taking place before, during, and after the wedding ceremony, and on different days. *Yerma* has to take place over a period of years to show the growing anguish of the protagonist. The first has a detailed plotline, the second a stylized one. *Bernarda Alba* takes place in a single home and is composed almost exclusively of dialogue among the characters. It is possible in the first two plays to estimate how much real time passes in the dramatic action. With *Bernarda Alba,* it is impossible to do so. Through effects of stage lighting, Lorca indicated one morning (act 1), one afternoon (act 2), and one evening (act 3). It is not important to an understanding of the structure to determine how much time passes between acts. Lorca guided the reader in understanding his intention in each play through his use of subtitles: *Blood Wedding* is a "tragedy," and *Yerma* a "tragic poem." He subtitled *Bernarda Alba,* "*Drama de mujeres en los pueblos de España*" ("Drama of Women in the Towns of Spain"), and the episodes in the play demonstrate the problems of women in the small towns of Spain. There are three acts, with no divisions into smaller *cuadros.*

The first act introduces the characters and the problems in the household. As the play opens, Bernarda Alba and her daughters are attending the funeral of the widow's second husband. Their absence allows La Poncia, the housekeeper, and the Maid (*Criada*) to give the reader their pictures of Bernarda Alba and her daughters before those characters appear onstage. Each episode, incident, character, conversation, and image contributes to a total understanding of the play. *Bernarda Alba* is Lorca's "tightest" work: not a word is wasted.

In the conversation between La Poncia and the Maid, most of the talk is about Bernarda; they paint a portrait of a virtual tyrant. Bernarda resents the fact that her help eats her food; she pulls out the hair of the housekeeper if the furniture does not shine; she keeps the Maid's hands bloody from work; and she keeps her mother locked up in a separate room. The family of her late husband hates her so much that none of them even came to the funeral. La Poncia believes that the late husband is better off dead than living with Bernarda. The Maid reveals that he was not entirely faithful to his wife; many were the times when he lifted the servant's skirt in the corral. Sexual references are pervasive in the play; in fact, sexual freedom is the play's theme (and will be the subject of a separate section of Chapter 6).

After the funeral, the women of the town fill Bernarda's house, pray together, and leave. The men are not allowed into the house. Before they go, the Girl (*Muchacha*) mentions that Pepe el Romano attended the funeral, a fact that Bernarda disputes much too much. As the women leave, Bernarda expresses the hope that it will be a long time before any of them sets foot in her house again. Bernarda's first few minutes on stage are a dramatic time. She screams "¡*Silencio!*" (Silence!) at the crying maid, likens the poor to animals, and throws a fit when Adela, her youngest daughter, offers her a fan unfit for a widow. She also announces that, following the tradition of her father's house, the family will observe eight years of mourning; during that time, not so much as a breath of fresh air will enter through a door or a window. The daughters will sit and embroider their trousseaux. Bernarda's next temper tantrum is directed against her eldest daughter, Angustias, who looked at and heard the conversation of men.

Finally, Bernarda and La Poncia are left alone. Theirs is an ambiguous relationship, somewhere between love and hate, between trust and self-interest. The scenes between them are among the most important in the play because the two women speak frankly with each other. They are also important in revealing La Poncia's real job in the family: she gathers the gossip about the neighbors that Bernarda can later use as emotional blackmail against them. Much of the gossip is of a sexual nature, and today's report is no exception. It involves Paca la Roseta, a woman who has moved to Bernarda's town and went off quite willingly the previous night with a group of men who tied up her husband and then took their pleasure with her.

The first conversation between two of the sisters reveals how Bernarda keeps the neighbors in fear of her by being the only person in possession of certain intimate facts about their lives. The reader also finds out that none of Bernarda's daughters has ever married because there are no men in town of their social position. Bernarda shows her true attitude toward charity by declaring that she will not give away so much as a button of her late husband's wardrobe.

The talk of the town today is that Pepe el Romano intends to ask Angustias to marry him. It appears that the only sister who has not yet heard the word is Adela, who can hardly contain her shock on learning the news. She cannot believe that the man is capable of doing that, but her sister Magdalena knows that he is capable of anything. On the Maid's announcement that Pepe is passing along the street, all of the sisters present (Angustias is not present) run to have a look at him. That move gets the sisters out of the room and leaves it free for Bernarda and La Poncia to speak again. The housekeeper reminds her employer of how much money Angustias (the daughter from her first marriage) has and how little the others have. Bernarda does not want to hear about it.

In the final segment of the act, Bernarda's mother, María Josefa, escapes from her room and enters the stage. She is adorned with flowers and wants to go out and get married instead of living in a houseful of frustrated old maids. She does not want to become like the rest of them; she wants to marry a handsome and virile man. She wants to be free. And so Bernarda has her locked up again, on a very strong first-act curtain.

Structure

The staging effects and dialogue reveal that act 2 takes place on a hot summer's afternoon. There is no reference to the funeral, and since one of the sisters, Martirio, admits that she could not sleep the night before because of the heat, there is the indication that the two acts do not occur on the same day. While the first act takes place in a room near the entrance to the Alba home, the second act takes place in a room that offers access to the sisters' bedrooms. The daughters are sitting and sewing. There is no indication of how much time has passed since the first act, but Angustias has now finished cutting the third bedsheet. When Magdalena asks if she should embroider Pepe's as well as Angustias's initials on the sheets, Angustias responds, oddly enough, in the negative. Adela is absent from the scene, still in bed, and La Poncia expresses concern for the youngest daughter's health. Martirio thinks that Adela's condition is no worse than that of all the sisters in the household: she needs a man. Only Angustias is free of that obsession. La Poncia mentions conversationally that she too was up during the night, and that at 1 A.M. Pepe was still talking with Angustias at her window. Amelia, another of the sisters, guesses that he left at 1:30 because she heard his cough and his horse's hooves. La Poncia thought she heard him leave as late as 4 A.M., which Angustias denies. La Poncia is able to offer the sisters what they do not get from their mother—a light word, a casual anecdote, a spicy story, and a quick change of subject when necessary.

When Adela arrives on the scene, she is in very bad spirits, complains of an aching body, and just wants to be left alone. Whenever the sisters ask her a question, she puts the worst face on it; they are not showing concern, as she sees it, they are being nosey. When the other sisters leave, Adela and La Poncia are left alone. Just as the housekeeper does not mince her words with Bernarda, neither does she do so with Adela. She suspects that Adela is in love with Pepe and that she might even be acting on her feelings. La Poncia's advice is that she not interfere with the forthcoming marriage between Pepe and Angustias, but that she also not give up hope of having him for herself someday. Angustias is sickly and will die in childbirth; then Pepe will marry the youngest and most attractive sister, who is Adela. Just as Bernarda puts La Poncia in her place when it is convenient for her to do so, so does Adela. She will not take La Poncia's advice, and she is not afraid of her—let the housekeeper say or do anything she wishes, Adela will act independently. Their argument comes to an abrupt halt when Angustias, followed shortly by the other sisters, enters the stage.

In the distance can be heard the sounds of 40 or 50 strong young men who have arrived for seasonal work in the fields. La Poncia warns the sisters to be careful not to leave the door ajar, because there is no telling what these strangers in the town are capable of doing. The sisters are jealous of the men's freedom to work, to sing, to be outdoors. Martirio can only look forward to the arrival of November and the end of the hot spell that the town is suffering. When Martirio and Amelia are left alone, their topic of conversation is the time Pepe leaves Angustias's window at night. Martirio is about to tell her sister something else on the subject but thinks better of doing so.

There is a sharp contrast in the play between the peaceful moments and the dramatic ones. The brief interlude between Amelia and Martirio comes to an end when Angustias storms furiously into the room and demands to know which one of her jealous sisters stole her picture of Pepe. Martirio insinuates that it was Adela. The loud argument attracts Bernarda to the scene. She has La Poncia search the daughters' rooms. When the housekeeper finds the picture between the sheets of Martirio's bed, Bernarda beats her daughter for what she has done.

Jealousies rage. Angustias does not feel responsible that Pepe has chosen her to be his wife, but Adela rubs her face in the fact that Pepe wants not her but her money. Martirio insinuates that someone in the house is engaged in more than just evil thoughts. Bernarda once again demands silence.

The following scene is between Bernarda and La Poncia and parallels the talk that they had in the first act. The housekeeper requests permission to speak frankly; Bernarda agrees because she knows that she may have an opportunity to get some information about what is going on under her own roof and about what the town is saying about her family, as well as an objective perspective on the situation. Also, she needs to unburden herself and to use La Poncia as a sounding board. Bernarda wants Angustias to get married as soon as possible, not so much to get Angustias out of the house as to get Pepe away from it. La Poncia warns Bernarda that there is a big problem in the house that will not go away: a storm is brewing in each sister's bedroom. Bernarda puts on her airs and denies that anything happens in her house that goes against her wishes; she then finds it convenient to shut up La Poncia by reminding her of her status in the household. In front of the daughters, neighbors, and servants, Bernarda is anxious to present the false picture of perfect bliss in her household. Just as La Poncia reveals to Bernarda that Pepe has been staying around until 4 A.M., Angustias bursts in to say that it is a lie. Martirio is quick to substantiate La Poncia's words.

There is another disturbance, noise in the street; Bernarda orders La Poncia to find out what is happening. It makes for juicy gossip: an unmarried woman had a baby, which she killed and buried to cover her shame. A dog uncovered the body, and now the town wants to see the woman punished for her sin. In an effective second-act curtain that at least equals that of the first act, Bernarda wants the punishment to take place before the police arrive by killing the woman in a manner that fits the crime: inserting burning coals in the part of the woman's body that is responsible for her sin. As Bernarda is screaming out for the sinner's death, Adela holds her own belly and begs for the town to have mercy and let the woman go free. Bernarda insists, "¡*Matadla!* ¡*Matadla!*" (1506; Kill her! Kill her!).

The third act takes place at night. Again the reader does not know how much time has passed between acts. The setting of the final act is a room in the back of the house with access to the corral. Bernarda, her daughters, and neighbor Prudencia have just finished dinner and what Prudencia calls a long visit. Despite Bernarda's earlier attitude about not having guests in her home, she is reluctant to see Prudencia leave. Bernarda pumps Prudencia for information about her husband, particularly about his relationship with their daughter. He has never forgiven his daughter for her actions during the distribution of an inheritance. His attitude is killing Prudencia, but Bernarda approves of it: he is acting like a real man. Bernarda is probably anxious to have her daughters hear her own statement that a daughter who disobeys her parents ceases to be a daughter and becomes instead an enemy. The conversation is disturbed by noises from the corral—a stallion is kicking to be let free. Bernarda orders that the horse be allowed out before he breaks down the walls, a freedom that she denies to her daughters.

The subject turns to Angustias's forthcoming marriage. Within three days, Pepe will formally ask for her hand. Prudencia has heard of what beautiful furniture Angustias has bought and admires her ring, although it is of pearls and not the traditional diamonds. At the sound of the last call for rosary prayers, Prudencia leaves, and Bernarda is alone with her daughters. One by one the others leave, and Bernarda is free to speak openly with Angustias.

This is the one tender scene in the play; Bernarda behaves as a caring mother. She wants Angustias to start speaking to Martirio again, despite the incident of the photograph. She even wants to hear about what Pepe has to say, which amounts to nothing: he always seems to be thinking about something (or someone) else. Bernarda has some motherly advice: Never pry into your husband's thoughts, and never let him see you cry. Don't look at him unless he looks at you first, don't talk to him unless he speaks first. Basically, stay out of his way. Bernarda is relieved that he will not be coming by that evening; the family can get to bed early and sleep peacefully. The other daughters return, and the momentary peace continues. Even Adela asks for motherly wisdom on the custom of reciting a poem to Saint Barbara on seeing a falling star.

Each preceding act contains a conversation between Bernarda and La Poncia, and this act is no exception. Bernarda needs information: Does the housekeeper's son still hear Pepe leaving the house at 4 A.M.? Are the townsfolk calling her house bad names? La Poncia claims to have heard nothing, and that satisfies Bernarda. La Poncia does advise Bernarda not to fall into a false sense of confidence; at any moment the worst can happen. All Bernarda wants to do is get to sleep.

The play opened with a scene between the Maid and the housekeeper, and now there is a similar dialogue. Once again they are speaking about Bernarda—about how blind she is to what is going on in her own home; about Adela—who may be doing more than just *talking* to Pepe; and about Martirio—who is the poison in the well. La Poncia knows that the situation has gone too far for peace to be reestablished.

The dogs bark, and Adela appears, allegedly to get a glass of water. In the midst of the noise, Bernarda's mother makes another appearance onstage. She has a lamb in her arms and is singing a lullaby to it. Adela is able to sneak out to the corral, but not Martirio, who is following her. Martirio stops to ask her grandmother where she is going. Where else would she want to go but out to get married and have children and be a part of the living world? She can no longer stand living in a houseful of old maids who will never have husbands but will be devoured by a man like Pepe el Romano.

Martirio catches Adela as she returns to the house from her tryst with Pepe. Martirio is less obsessed with Angustias, who is going to marry Pepe, than with Adela, who is enjoying him. They argue, and Martirio calls out for Bernarda. Martirio shows Bernarda the straw on the disheveled Adela's nightgown, the sign of her sin. Bernarda shoots at Pepe, and Martirio leads Adela to believe that their mother has killed him. In fact, Pepe rides off on his horse. What had seemed like a casual reference earlier in the act to what a dark night it is turns out to be not so incidental after all. It is the darkness of the night that keeps Bernarda from hitting her mark.

By now the entire household is awake, including La Poncia. Bernarda hears a crash behind the door into which Adela has escaped, and she has the housekeeper investigate. Adela has hanged herself. Bernarda's reaction is to have La Poncia dress Adela in white and to announce that she died a virgin. As for the rest of the family, "Silence!"

The circular structure of the play is virtually flawless. The drama begins with Bernarda returning from one funeral and ends with her arranging another. She begins her first entrance with the demand "Silence!" and ends the last act with the same word. There is a significant difference, however, in the power of the word at the beginning and end of the play. Her first utterance of it is authoritarian; the last time is hollow, for now the town is awakened, and the implication is that the secrets of the house of Bernarda Alba will now become public knowledge. Examinations of the roles of the characters, images, and techniques will reveal how each complements the others to form a perfectly structured play.

chapter 5

Characters

The plots of Lorca's plays may be simple, but his characters are not. They are the heart and lifeblood of his drama. Lorca paid minimal attention to the details of their physical appearance but delved deep into their minds and souls to depict their motivations and strife. He gave the reader and audience a picture of every facet of their lives rather than just those pertinent to the moments of conflict in the plays. In that respect, Lorca followed in the footsteps of both the Greek tragedians and such classical European playwrights as Corneille and Racine.

As Lorca listed the characters in *Blood Wedding,* they fall into one of three categories: first, all of the women (including such minor characters as the Neighbor and the Girls); then the men; and finally the symbolic or metaphoric characters. Since Lorca listed the Mother first, it is with her that this chapter will begin. Typical of Lorquian heroines, the Mother is an obsessed character, and to say so is not to criticize her: her life has been dominated and controlled by two tragedies. At some time in the past, before the play begins, her husband and elder son were killed with knives at the hands of members of the Félix clan. Those tragedies have given the Mother three driving passions in life: hate and a desire for revenge against the Félixes, protectiveness and a desire to shelter her only surviving son from disaster, and a dread of knives. The intensity of her feeling is revealed in her choppy speech at the beginning of the play (which appears in the previous chapter and establishes the mood for the entire drama). The lines that follow those quoted in Chapter 4 reveal the essential aspects of the Mother's personality. She is concerned with her son's well-being and therefore wants to give him something to eat; in addition, she curses the knives that killed her other son and husband.

NOVIO:	¿Quieres algo?
MADRE:	Hijo, el almuerzo.
NOVIO:	Déjalo. Comeré uvas. Dame la navaja.
MADRE:	¿Para qué?
NOVIO:	(Riendo.) Para cortarlas.
MADRE:	(Entre dientes y buscándola.) La navaja, la navaja. . . . Malditas sean todas y el bribón que las inventó. (1172)
(BRIDEGROOM:	What is it?
MOTHER:	Son, your lunch.
BRIDEGROOM:	Leave it, I'll eat grapes. Give me the knife.
MOTHER:	What for?
GROOM:	[Laughing.] To cut them.
MOTHER:	[Muttering and looking for it.] The knife, the knife. Damn them all and the scoundrel who invented them.)

The Mother is a highly poetic character, a trait that she reveals when she describes the destructive power of knives, which can cut down a man in the prime of his life as he goes to his work in the vineyards. Once the Mother is reminded of her tragedy, it dominates her thoughts. If she lives 100 years, she will not speak about anything else; after all, she lost her husband after only three years of marriage, and then her son. Her losses explain her protective attitude toward her only living son. She does, however, go overboard in wishing that he were a girl who could sit at home with her and sew. She also laments the fact that after his marriage her son will be moving out and leaving her alone. She refuses to move in with her son because she will not leave the spot where her husband and son died and are buried.

The Mother has an innate distrust of her son's future wife even before she learns that the woman once had a fiancé who is a Félix: there is just something about the woman, whom she has never met, that makes her uncomfortable. The Mother does not trust a woman who has had more than one boyfriend or who has looked at more than one man. All women should have her attitudes. "*Yo no miré a nadie. Miré a tu padre, y cuando lo mataron miré a la pared de enfrente. Una mujer con un hombre, y ya está*" (1176; I didn't look at anyone. I looked at your father, and when they killed him I looked at the wall in front of me. One woman with one man, and that's that). She shows just how traditional she is in her comment, "*Los hombres, hombres; el trigo, trigo*" (1174; Men are men, wheat is wheat). Bernarda Alba will make a similar remark. However, the Mother does consent to meet the young woman and to bring her a gift of a family heirloom, and she wants her son to buy gifts for his bride. The Mother contents herself momentarily with the thought that at least she will be blessed with half a dozen grandchildren.

It is only moments later that the Neighbor confirms the suspicion that the young woman did in fact have a former boyfriend, a Félix. The Mother ignores the fact that the man was only an eight-year-old child at the time of the murder of her husband and son. She alternately spits and crosses herself at the mention of the name of Félix and at the thought of her son's future and her family's tragic past.

If the Mother is uneasy at the opening of the play and distressed by the news of the former boyfriend, she is on edge when she has to enter the cave where the Bride lives with her father. Her conversation with the Father is to the point: she wants nothing from him, and when she dies the children should sell her land and buy the piece that adjoins the land where they will be living. She wants no small talk, just to hear about the arrangements for the marriage. She presents her son honestly and, as she believes, in the best possible light: he has never known a woman and has unblemished honor. When she learns of the Bride's domesticity, she is willing to bless the union. She has a bit of advice about marriage for the bride-to-be: *"Un hombre, unos hijos y una pared de dos varas de ancho para todo lo demás"* (1200; One man, some children, and a thick wall separating you from everything else). When she hears the Bride accept her advice, she offers her the gifts.

At the wedding, the Mother is surprised to see Leonardo and his wife. Her remark to the Father is revealing: *"Me aguanto, pero no perdono"* (1221; I put up, but I don't forgive). She further says that Leonardo cannot be any good because the blood in his veins is that of his ancestors. When she looks at him, she can see only the hand of death that his family put on hers. She remembers how she bloodied her own hands on the body of her dead son.

She does her best to be kind to the Bride on the day of the wedding but cannot help noticing that the Bride's mood does not reflect the occasion. For the Mother, her wedding day was the only good day of her life. *"Es la roturación de las tierras, la plantación de árboles nuevos."* (1240; It is the plowing of new lands, the planting of new trees). She has words of motherly advice for her son:

> *Con tu mujer procura estar cariñoso, y si la notas infautada o arisca, hazle una caricia que le produzca un poco de daño, un abrazo fuerte, un mordisco y luego un beso suave. Que ella no pueda disgustarse, pero que sienta que tú eres el macho, el amo, el que mandas."* (1241; With your wife, try to be affectionate, and if you see that she is unpleasant or surly, give her a caress that hurts her a little, a strong hug, a nibble and then a soft kiss. Don't let her become disgusted, but make her know that you are the man, the boss, the one who rules).

When she learns from Leonardo's wife that her daughter-in-law has run off with Leonardo, she takes a firm position and orders her son to go after them. In the final irony of the play, after her son and Leonardo kill each other, the Mother is bereft of kin, hopeless about the continuation of her line, and in the constant company of the

woman who caused the final blow to her life. Her actions at the end
of the play foreshadow the two plays yet to come. As Yerma, she is a
woman without children or the hope of ever having them again. As
Bernarda Alba, she slaps the Bride and tells her to keep quiet. She does
not want to hear of her purity or to see her tears; she wants only to
be left alone in her misery.

The Bride is probably a more important character than either the
Bridegroom or Leonardo, but an understanding of the two men—
especially the differences between them—helps to explain her actions
in the play. Lorca has been praised for the depth of feeling that he
depicts in his female characters and criticized for the shallowness of
his male characters. That dichotomy is nowhere better demonstrated
than in *Blood Wedding*.[1] The men exist on the physical level but seem
to have no psychological dimension. In addition, the contrast between
the Bridegroom and Leonardo shows how precisely the men in Lorca's
theater fall into two broad categories: they are either weak and emotionally ineffectual, or strong and sensual.

The Bridegroom is a wholesome young man and that is his problem, at least from the point of view of the Bride. The Bridegroom
allows himself to be defined by his mother, whom he assures he will
always obey. There is no question that she loves her son deeply and is
entirely devoted to him. But she does him no favors by telling him that
she wishes he were a girl, by telling the Father of the Bride (in front
of the Bride) that he has never known another woman (in a sexual
sense), or by pointedly telling the Father that her son never touches
wine. She does not even allow the son to refuse the drink for himself;
she speaks for him. In Spanish society, it is entirely permissible to drink
wine and for a man to have had sexual relations with other women
before his marriage. We learn from the Father that his son-in-law-to-
be is a physically strong man, and we know that he has broad shoulders. But his strength ends there. As portrayed by the Bride, he is ineffectual as a lover. The Bridegroom is a woman-dominated man.
When he outgrows the control of his mother, it is replaced by the
manipulation of his bride, to whom he is little more than a pawn. He
is also indecisive. It takes his mother to order him to go after his new

wife when she leaves him; all his search produces for him, however, is his death. It is of little consolation, but perhaps of some significance, that he does kill Leonardo, who also kills him. There are moments when he shows himself capable of being romantic with his moody, future wife. "*Cuando me voy de tu lado siento un despego grande y así como un nudo en la garganta*" (1202; When I leave your side I feel a great coolness and a lump in my throat). The Bride is quick to thwart his warm intentions. Again, on the night of the wedding, he tries to learn what is bothering his new wife, only to be rebuffed by her. The Bridegroom is not important as a character in and of himself. He exists as the physical embodiment of all that the Mother has left in life until she loses him, too. And he serves to explain the character of the Bride, especially when he is contrasted with Leonardo.

If the Bridegroom comes across as a less-than-perfect lover for the Bride (she never gives him a chance), it is because Leonardo is the very picture of virility. Leonardo is as irresponsible (especially as a husband) as the Bridegroom is reliable. Leonardo also has the distinction of being the only character in the play with a proper name; he is not described in terms of his function or relationship with another character. His problem is that he is married to the wrong woman. He had been the Bride's boyfriend, but they never married, perhaps because he thought the woman who did become his wife was a more appropriate choice. She is submissive and wholly devoted to him. And he does not deserve her, which is made clear from his first appearance in the play. It is during that moment that his wife reveals to him that the Bride is going to be married within the next month. He takes the news poorly, and with good reason. There is every indication that the time he spends away from his wife and job he spends with the Bride; naturally, he is reluctant to give his wife straightforward answers to simple questions about his whereabouts. The tenderness that he does not have for his wife, he does have for his son. In fact, it is about the baby that he asks when he enters the stage, not about his wife's well-being. He also has another good trait: he is just as hard-working as the Bridegroom (and Juan and Víctor in *Yerma*) in his field of horseshoeing—a most appropriate trade for him (as the section on images will reveal).

Characters

Unfortunately, he is still obsessed with the Bride, though their relationship supposedly ended three years before. Not only does he accept the invitation to her wedding, he is the first to arrive—and alone: he refused to ride by carriage with his wife and so came on horseback, a far more masculine way to travel. He reveals to the Bride that he has never gotten over their breakup: "*Después de mi casamiento he pensado noche y día de quién era la culpa, y cada vez que pienso sale una culpa nueva que se come a la otra; pero siempre hay culpa*" (1214; Since my marriage I have thought night and day about whose fault it was [that they broke up], and every time that I think about it a different fault arises that negates the last one that I thought of; but there is always the guilt).

What is certain is that Leonardo's passion for the Bride has never abated. Even in front of the Maid, he says as much as he can about his constant preoccupation with his former girlfriend. He does finally promise the Maid that this is the last time he will ever speak to the Bride; the promise is short-lived, however, for soon after the wedding ceremony takes place, he and the Bride run off together. The breaking of his promise costs him his life, and he thereby fulfills the promise that he made to the Bride in the third act—that if they are ever separated it will be because he is dead.

The next character in the play worthy of study is the Bride. In effect, her actions bring about the final tragedies, and she is the character on whom the theme of the play may well be centered. The Bride is presented to the readers first through indirect introduction—other characters talking about her—and then by direct presentation—speaking and acting for herself. The reader's first impressions of her are quite favorable. The Mother is certain that the Bride "*es buena. . . . Modosa. Trabajadora.*" (1175; is a good girl. . . . Well-behaved. A hard worker). The Neighbor, too, has good things to say about her: "*¡Buena muchacha! [pero] quien la conozca a fondo no hay nadie*" (1180; A good girl! [but] there is nobody who knows her deeply). There is some kind of mystery that surrounds her. She is 22 years old and lives with her father far from the nearest neighbor; she is accustomed to solitude. The one possible blemish on her character is that she had a boyfriend three years before. She is modest and respectful during the visit of the Bridegroom and the Mother to her cave. She assures the Mother that she will live within the strictest and most traditional definition of marriage.

Her true feelings emerge when she is left alone with the Maid. Her irritability betrays more than the apprehensions of a bride-to-be. The whole subject of the approaching wedding is upsetting to her. She is also not pleased to see Leonardo appear at her wedding; she knows herself well enough to realize that it is dangerous for her even to speak to him. She stops him in his tracks when he tries to approach her. After the wedding ceremony, she is just as standoffish with the man who is now her husband. His every approach receives an uncivil response: she claims not to feel well, she wishes to rest, she wants only to be left alone. The suggestion that her husband accompany her to her bedroom while she rests is repulsive to her; she claims to be concerned about what people will say. Perhaps she has already made up her mind to run off with Leonardo. When the Bride and Leonardo are making their way through the woods, Leonardo reminds her that it was she who initiated the flight. Her devotion to him is so deep, she says, that

> Y yo dormiré a tus pies
> para guardar lo que sueñas.
> Desnuda, mirando al campo,
> (Dramática.)
> Como si fuera una perra,
> ¡porque eso soy! Que te miro
> y tu hermosura me quema. (1259)

> (I'll sleep at your feet
> to guard your dreams.
> Naked, watching the fields,
> [*Dramatically.*]
> as if I were a dog.
> because that is what I am! I see you
> and your beauty burns me.)

It is in the final scene with her mother-in-law that she reveals her motivations and contrasts the two men in her life:

Characters

Yo era una mujer quemada, llena de llagas por dentro y por fuera,
y tu hijo era un poquito de agua de lo que yo esperaba hijos, tierra,
salud; pero el otro era un río oscuro, lleno de ramas, que acercaba
a mí el rumor de sus juncos y su cantar entre dientes. Y yo corría
con tu hijo que era un niñito de agua, frío y el otro me mandaba
cientos de pájaros que me impedían el andar y que dejaban escarcha
sobre mis heridas de pobre mujer marchita, de muchacha acariciada
por el fuego. Yo no quería, ¡óyelo bien!; yo no quería, ¡óyelo!, yo
no quería. Tu hijo era mi fin y yo no lo he engañado, pero el brazo
del otro me arrastró como un golpe de mar, como la cabezada de
un mulo, y me hubiera arrastrado siempre, siempre, siempre,
aunque hubiera sido vieja y todos los hijos de tu hijo me hubiesen
agarrado de los cabellos. (1269)

(I was a woman on fire, full of pain both inside and out, and your
son was a little drop of water from which I had hoped to get children, land, health; but the other was a dark river, full of tributaries,
from which I heard the sound of his bullrushes and the song between his teeth. And there I was going off with your son, a baby-
sized drop of water, cold, and the other was sending out hundreds
of birds that blocked my path and left frost on the wounds of this
poor, withered woman, a girl caressed by fire. I didn't want to, listen
and listen well, I didn't want to, I didn't want to! Your son was my
end in life, and I never deceived him; but the arm of the other
dragged me like the force of the sea, like being kicked by a mule
and he would have dragged me along forever, forever, even after I
had become old and all of your son's children had pulled at my
hair.)

The Bride's crime or sin is that she wanted to fulfill her passions and
satisfy her desire for the man she loved. As a result, two men are dead,
and she and her mother-in-law are condemned to a lifetime of
remembering.

The most perceptive character in the play is the Bride's maid. It is
she who notices that the Bride's attitude is not appropriate for a
woman about to be married and who discovers that the Bride has
never renounced Leonardo, although he is now a husband and father.
The Maid's suspicions are aroused when the Bride reacts so extremely
to the Maid's simple request to see her wedding gifts. The Maid ob-

serves, "*Parece como si no tuvieras ganas de casarte*" (1203; It seems as if you didn't want to get married). It is also the Maid who previously heard Leonardo's horse at the Bride's home. In the second act, it is apparent that the more the Maid talks of the joys of marriage, the more annoyed the Bride becomes. It may well be the Maid's intention to bring the problem to a head. When Leonardo arrives for the wedding, there is a definite tension between him and the Maid. The Maid changes the subject when Leonardo asks the Bride if she is happy, does not allow the Bride to speak about the past with Leonardo, and finally has to order him out of the Bride's presence. She also knows when *not* to drop a subject, such as when the Father of the Bride dismisses as trivial the fact that Leonardo is at the wedding. The Maid appears in one form or another in each of the plays of the trilogy and is a unifying element running through the three plays.

Brief notes are in order on Leonardo's wife and the Neighbor. The former is a woman neglected by an insensitive and disregarding husband. She serves to introduce the plight of Yerma, the most neglected and emotionally starved wife in Lorca's dramatic creation. The Neighbor serves as the messenger, as in Greek tragedy. It is she who first breaks the news to the Mother that the Bride was once involved with Leonardo, a Félix. There are other characters in the play worthy of consideration such as the Moon, the Beggar Woman, and the Woodcutters. Since they are dramatic techniques and images more than characters, they will be discussed in Chapter 6.

If it is challenging to establish a time frame for the play, it is even more difficult to determine who is the tragic hero or heroine. It could be Leonardo, whose arrogance led him to abandon his wife and child to run off with a married woman. Perhaps it is the Bridegroom, whose naïveté makes him ignore his mother's advice and his family's history in his decision to marry the Bride. Maybe it is one of the women: the Bride, whose sexual passion drove her into the arms of another man on her wedding night; or maybe the Mother, left alone in the world after the death of her husband and two sons, except for the continuous presence of the Bride, a constant reminder of the tragedies in her life. There is good reason to believe that Lorca intended the Mother to be the tragic heroine, since he reserved that role in the original production for Margarita Xirgu, the actress he designated for the lead role in so many of his plays, including *Mariana Pineda, The Shoemaker's Prodigious Wife, Yerma,* and *The House of Bernarda Alba.*

Yerma is the main character in the play that bears her name. The other characters exist only to highlight her and heighten the intensity of her struggle. Yerma has a singleness of purpose in life: she wants—no, needs—to be a mother, and that driving passion blinds her to all reason. This play about a barren woman represents Lorca's best integration of character, theme, and imagery, all of which are inherent in the heroine's name: *Yerma* means *barren.* The play traces her ever-growing desperation to be fulfilled as a woman and to be a part of life, of the world of nature in which everything and everyone has a purpose, that of reproducing.

Yerma is the victim of a set of circumstances from which there is no escape. In part, the circumstances are outside forces imposed by others; in part, they are self-imposed by her rigid standard of decency. There are certain aspects of her life over which she has no control—most importantly, the man to whom she is married. They are a couple incapable of producing a child together. Lorca was careful not to place the blame for Yerma's barren state on either the husband or the wife. In the mythic society in which they live, a child is the product of more than a mere physical act; it is the result of an act of love between a husband and a wife. Some critics have tried to call Juan impotent; but if he is, it is emotional, not physical, impotence. For him to be impotent would be to ruin the mystery that Lorca insisted accompanies the process of becoming pregnant.

Yerma had no choice in the man she was to marry; her father had picked Juan, and she had obediently married him. Yerma even believes, at least at the beginning of the play, that she loves her husband. She recalls that the first time she went into his bed, she did not hesitate or cry, as other young brides do. She accepted him willingly; she went so willingly that her mother cried at Yerma's lack of regret over leaving her home. She is also willing—again, at the beginning of the play—to embrace and kiss Juan; Lorca specified that the acts of affection are initiated by her.

Yerma tries to be a good wife, at least as much as she can. Before

October 1937 production of *Bodas de sangre*. Margarita Xirgu, in the role of Madre, is dressed in black (act 1, scene 3). *Courtesy of the Fundación Federico García Lorca.*

Juan leaves for work in the fields, Yerma offers him a glass of milk to give him nourishment. Her offer may well be self-serving: if Juan nourishes his body, perhaps he will have the physical stamina to make Yerma a mother. She would also like to see Juan go up to the roof and take in the sun so that he would not be so pale. That is another ploy to strengthen Juan enough to impregnate her. To Yerma, Juan is sick and needs personal care.

If Yerma's obsession with having a child is foreign to Juan, so is her language, which is highly poetic. She uses imagery out of nature, and Juan has little time or patience for it. Yerma sees the function of each detail in nature. For example, she criticizes those who say that *jaramago* plants serve no purpose; she sees that they produce yellow flowers that sway in the air. In other words, they add beauty to the world.

Yerma has no doubt that her husband loves her enough for them to be able to produce a child, so she asks her neighbor María, who is pregnant, if her husband loves her. María does not know—how would she? Does a man in a mythical-Spanish-macho society keep telling his wife how much he loves her? Of course not. But her husband does not have to tell her. Her pregnancy is the proof of his love. And there are other physical signs, too: "*Se pone junto a mí y sus ojos tiemblan como dos hojas verdes*" (1281; He gets close to me and his eyes tremble like two green leaves). Now that María has the good fortune of being pregnant, Yerma wants her to take care of the baby even before it leaves her body. In Yerma's characteristically poetic style, she tells María to breathe gently, as if she had a rose between her teeth.

There is a great difference between Yerma's and María's knowledge about love, sex, and pregnancy; Yerma's is studied, while María's is intuitive. And that is Yerma's problem in a nutshell; she lacks spontaneity, she behaves mechanically. She has done everything that is physically necessary to have a child, but she has not done what is spiritually or emotionally necessary. She does not "sing" in bed with her husband, she does not rejoice in him and in the sexual act. She performs it because she must to become a mother. In other words, Yerma and Juan are equally at fault. They do not "make love": they merely use each other's body—he, for the physical release and performance of his marital obligation; she, with her mind on having a child, thereby making of her husband a tool, an instrument of impregnation, a sperm machine. She regrets the fact that she cannot become pregnant alone.

Yerma does not always blame Juan for her infecund state. Alternately, she accepts the responsibility. She wishes she were a woman and speaks of herself as if she were a man. She even thinks that her footsteps sound like those of a man. She walks barefoot through the fields hoping that the telluric forces of fecundity will enter her body through osmosis. And she goes to Dolores the conjurer to become pregnant through the power of black magic.

It is not only the external conditions that keep her barren; some of the fault must be attributed to her strong sense of personal honor, which will not allow her to turn to a man other than her husband—

Víctor, for example, or the son of the Old Woman at the pagan fertility rite. She is less controlled by the gossip that might spring up about her and put her name on the tongues of the women of the region than she is by the possibility of betraying her own personal standards of decency and self-respect. She categorically rejects Juan's suggestion of raising a relative's child to fulfill her maternal needs because she needs more than a child to rear. She needs the entire physiological process of becoming pregnant, carrying the child, and having it be a product of her blood.

She has no other option in life than to have a child with her husband, and therefore she views life as essentially unfair. Every other married woman in town is a mother except Yerma, while it is she who has the strongest maternal desires, perhaps because they have been frustrated for so long. She engages in a good deal of self-pity, all to no avail. She believes that every woman's body contains enough blood for four or five children and that if a woman does not have those children her blood will turn to poison, as will happen to hers. She speaks of herself in Christological terms of bearing her cross and taking the nails.[2] She feels psychologically, spiritually, and emotionally poor and believes that her complaints are justified. She says to María, "¡*Cómo no me voy a quejar cuando te veo a ti y a otras mujeres llenas por dentro de flores, y viéndome yo inútil en medio de tanta hermosura!*" (1317; How can I not complain when I see you and other women filled from within with flowers, and I see myself useless and surrounded by so much beauty!).

Part of the reason for her grief is the romantic terms in which she sees children. To her mind, the pain that they can cause is really pleasure in disguise. She begs for a child to make her suffer so that her "blind" breasts can come to and offer life. She thinks that women who say that they suffer because of their children are weak and whining. "*Tener un hijo no es tener un ramo de rosas. Hemos de sufrir para verlos crecer*" (1283; To have a child is not to have a bouquet of roses. We have to suffer to see them grow). At the core of the problem is the fact that Yerma feels useless, low, fed up, and offended that she is not a part of the life going on all around her. Her problem is so extreme that she is overwhelmed by it. She knows that "*lo tendré [un hijo] porque lo tengo que tener. O no entiendo el mundo*" (1328; I'll have [a child] because I have to have one. Or I do not understand the world). It just isn't fair.[3]

If Yerma's problem is that she is married to the wrong man, Juan's is that he is married to the wrong woman. While she wants maternity, he wants tranquillity. As she agonizes over the absence of children in the house, he revels in the fact that he does not have to spend his hard-earned cash to support them. It is clear that until Juan wants children Yerma will not be able to have them. Juan is essentially a good husband and provider, and Yerma complains about just those traits. She admits that he gives her food and shelter and laments the fact that he *is* so good. What he is good at is prospering the work of his hands. He does not mean to be unkind or unfair to his wife, he just does not understand her. He does not know what else she needs or why she keeps complaining.

What he gives to his land he fails to give to his wife: attention and, yes, cultivation. He spends the night irrigating the fields to make them productive, while his wife remains alone in bed wishing that he were making *her* productive, or rather, reproductive. If Yerma's deal in life is unfair, so is Juan's. He needs a wife who is as tradition-bound as he is, who speaks in simple terms, and who can appreciate the good husband that she has in him. What he has is a wife who is constantly calling his masculinity into question and who has made him the object of the town's gossip through her strange behavior. A good wife stays at home; she does not talk to other men, go walking through the fields barefoot, meet with witches, or attend fertility rites. As Juan sees it— and from his point of view, he is correct—Yerma has robbed him of his honor. Yerma's and Juan's concepts of honor are different, and there are two different words in Spanish to describe them. Yerma is concerned with *honra,* which is an internal sense of personal dignity; Juan worries about *honor,* the prestige that comes from others. Their two different concepts of honor are mutually offensive to each other. When Juan accuses Yerma of having robbed him of his *honor,* he is offending her sense of *honra.* Yerma goes about talking of her problem to anyone who will listen and potentially be a source of advice. She refers to Juan as *frío* (cold) and *blanco* (pale), qualities not associated with virility.

Most women would be thrilled with what Juan offers Yerma, beyond the food and shelter. He wants her for herself and not as a means to any other end. His desire for her—only her—is what costs him his life. Yerma will not have what should be an act of production—again, reproduction—reduced to an act of simple physical need and pleasure, and she will not give him her affection if there is no baby in the offing. One might be tempted to write on the play from Juan's point of view— how it feels to be the husband of a nagging wife who constantly challenges his masculinity. To do so, however, would be to deny Lorca's stated purpose in writing the play: the tragedy of the barren women.[4]

Except for the fact that both Juan and Víctor are hard-working and financially successful, they share no other qualities. In fact, they serve in *Yerma* the same contrast that the Bridegroom and Leonardo serve in *Blood Wedding*. Lorca gave every indication in the text that if Yerma had married Víctor, she would have been a mother. Yerma's situation relative to the two men in the play roughly parallels that of the Bride in *Blood Wedding*. Had the Bride married Leonardo, her amorous and sexual desires would have been fulfilled; had Yerma married Víctor, she would have fulfilled her maternal desires.

Víctor is everything that Juan is not. Juan is cold and pale, Víctor is warm and tan; Juan is serious, Víctor is cheerful. Even his voice is that of a flood of water. (Chapter 7 will make clear the relationship between water and virility.) Just by being in Víctor's presence, Yerma can "hear" a baby. Furthermore, the only time Yerma ever "trembled" (with sexual or amorous joy) in a man's presence was when Víctor held her in his arms. Yerma's feelings when she is around Víctor only heighten her sense of frustration about her barren state: things could have been different from what they are. Víctor's announcement that he is moving to another area is another blow to Yerma. Although she could never have considered being unfaithful to her husband, she does admit to Víctor that neither of them knows what the future might have held in store. Víctor's leaving, Juan's accusations, his sisters' haunting, and her neighbors gossiping about her make Yerma believe that her situation has become hopeless.

Two other characters in *Yerma* deserve comment. The Old Woman to whom Yerma turns for advice is reminiscent of the Maid in *Blood Wedding* and a forerunner of La Poncia and María Josefa in *Bernarda Alba*. She is a perceptive woman who impresses Yerma with her learned air and who, despite her advanced age, believes that she still has many years ahead of her. As the Mother in *Blood Wedding,* she is devoted to and takes care of her adult son.

The character who is a real thorn in Yerma's side is the Second Girl. She is a character who flies in the face of the values of her society. She does not want to have children and did not even want to get married, but first marriage and now children are being imposed on her by her mother Dolores. She complains about the turn her life has taken. "*Yo tengo diecinueve años y no me gusta guisar ni lavar. Bueno; pues todo el día he de estar haciendo lo que no me gusta. ¿Y para qué? ¿Qué necesidad tiene mi marido de ser mi marido? Porque lo mismo hacíamos de novio que ahora*" (1293; I am 19 years old and I don't like to cook or wash. Well, now I have to spend the whole day doing what I don't like to do. And why? Why does my husband have to be my husband? We did the same thing as boyfriend and girlfriend that we do now).

Lorca stated that *Yerma* was to be a four-character play enhanced by choruses. It is easy enough to identify three of the characters— Yerma, Juan, and Víctor—but who is the fourth? Is it María, who gives birth; or the Old Woman, who speculates on Juan's guilt; or Dolores, who acts as a sorceress for sterile women; or the Second Girl, who prefers not being a wife and mother? That fourth character may very well be one who, like Pepe in *Bernarda Alba,* does not have an active role in the play. It may be the Child who appears only in the dream sequence of the opening scene and with whom Yerma later engages in a poetic dialogue in one of the songs.

The choice of the Child is more logical than may seem immediately apparent, but the roles of other children in Lorca's theater should be considered. The lullaby to the baby in *Blood Wedding* presents the themes and imagery that will dominate the rest of the play. The children in the wedding scene are the chorus singing to the Bride and representing the voices of society and tradition. In *Bernarda Alba*, it is a child who introduces the name of Pepe el Romano. The theme of children dominates *Yerma*, just as children preoccupy Yerma.

Margarita Xirgu said that Lorca wrote *The House of Bernarda Alba* because she asked him to create a role that would give her a chance to play a "hard" woman after her portrayal of the lonely old maid in *Rosie the Spinster*. She also said that the playwright wanted *Bernarda Alba* to have its opening in Buenos Aires.

While it is debatable whether Bernarda Alba is the principal character in the play that bears her name, her presence is certainly pervasive. For Sherwood Collins, Bernarda is a dramatic descendant of Medea.[5] After two marriages and the deaths of both husbands, Bernarda is the widowed mother of five adult daughters. Her first marriage produced Angustias, and her second Magdalena, Amelia, Martirio, and Adela.

The conversation in the first act between the housekeeper and the Maid, even before Bernarda makes her first appearance on the stage, establishes the fact that Bernarda has always been a vicious and manipulative person who keeps a mental record of every scandal that involves her neighbors so that she can use the information as a psychological weapon against them. Her domination seems to intensify on the day of the funeral of her second husband. She enters the scene demanding silence: the Maid should not be spending her time crying over the dead, she should be working. And her behavior just becomes worse as the act continues. When the Girl dares mention that she saw Pepe el Romano, Angustias's intended, at the funeral, Bernarda snaps back that the man she and everyone else saw was the widower Darajalí getting very close to the Girl's aunt, and that ends that. After the ritualistic *Requiem aeternam donat eis Domine,* Bernarda orders the neighbors out of her house and expresses the wish, "¡*Ojalá tardéis muchos años en pasar el arco de mi puerta!*" (1450; May many years pass before you enter my doorway again!).

Insulated from the spying eyes of the women of the town, Bernarda is free to order her daughters about and establish the law that will prevail in her home. "*En ocho años que dure el luto no ha de entrar en esta casa el viento de la calle. Hacemos cuenta que hemos tapiado con ladrillos puertas y ventanas. Así pasó en casa de mi padre y en casa de mi abuelo. Mientras podéis empezar a bordar el ajuar.*" (1451; In the eight years that the mourning will last not even the breeze from the street must enter this house. . . . That's how things were in my father's and grandfather's homes. Meanwhile, you can begin to embroider your trousseaux). Bernarda fails to see the contradiction in what she has just said: Why do her daughters need a hope chest? What have they to hope for during the next eight years? How can they expect to meet future husbands if they are not allowed to leave the house or to invite men into it?

A conflict immediately arises between Bernarda and Adela, her youngest and most rebellious daughter. When Bernarda requests a fan, Adela gives her one designed with red and green flowers. Bernarda goes into a fury over her daughter's lack of consideration for a widow: the fan should be solid black, to show respect for the dead. And yet when Magdalena, the only daughter who loved her father, and who fainted from grief during the funeral, cries for her late father, Bernarda warns her, "*Magdalena, no llores; si quieres llorar te metes debajo de la cama*" (1446; Magdalena, don't cry; if you want to cry go under the bed [to do it]). Bernarda is dominated by her fatalistic view of life and her stoic philosophy. She has no illusions of what it is to be a woman, whose role she believes it is to suffer. She later reminds her daughters that she will control every detail of their lives and spy on their every movement for as long as she lives.

Bernarda is motivated by two obsessions: social class and decency. Now that there is no man in the house, she must be mercilessly vigilant to see that her family not be involved in a scandal and that the names of her daughters not find their way to the tongues of her neighbors. She may control her household, but her fear of the *quedirán* (gossip) controls her.

Aside from having to live in isolation for the next eight years, Bernarda's daughters (except for Angustias) have no chance of marrying because there are no men in the town who are of Bernarda's social position. She rejects as out of order La Poncia's suggestion that she move to a town where there are men who would be acceptable to her as candidates for marriage to her daughters, since such an act would be "selling" them. What she really fears about moving to another town is that she would no longer be the rich one whom all others in the town must respect. She would also lose the advantage of having the gossip, gathered over a lifetime, with which to control them. Martirio once had a chance at marriage with Enrique Humanas, but Bernarda let him know that he had better not appear to court her daughter. "*Su padre fue gañán*" (1498; His father was a wage-earner). Inextricably bound up with Bernarda's social pretensions is her concern about money, especially in her widowhood when there is no man to provide for her or her daughters. She is fully aware that, of her five eligible daughters, only Angustias has the economic resources to attract a man.

The other motivating force in her life is decency. She is determined that her daughters will conduct themselves in such a way that they can never become the subject of gossip; she will not have the townspeople controlling her through blackmail, as she does them. Bernarda takes her most frightening stand in the name of decency in the strong curtain that ends the second act. A single woman has given birth and killed the child in an attempt to hide her shame. The people of the town are outraged and want to kill her. Bernarda is adamant and wants her to pay the wages of sin: "*Y que pague la que pisotea la decencia*" (1505; And let her who trespasses upon decency pay). Bernarda is determined to see not only that the young woman die but that she do so in the most painful and humiliating manner possible. She is determined to set an example for the other women of the town in general and for her own daughters in particular.

Both preoccupations, social class and decency, come into play in Bernarda's reaction to Angustias in the first act. When Bernarda learns from Adela that Angustias was standing in the doorway as the men were leaving Bernarda's patio, the mother is furious. "*¿Es decente que una mujer de tu clase vaya con el anzuelo detrás de un homre el día* *de la misa de su padre?*" (1454; Is it decent for a woman of your class to lure the attention of a man on the day of her father's funeral mass?). Bernarda advances and beats her daughter as she calls her a tramp. Later in the same act, Angustias incurs her mother's wrath when she appears made up and wishes to go out for a walk.

Is Bernarda a villain or a good mother trying to protect the reputation of her daughters? She sees herself, of course, as the latter. She reminds herself as she speaks to La Poncia (whom she alternately takes into her confidence and holds in contempt), "¡*Tendré que sentarles la mano! Bernarda: acuérdate que esta es tu obligación*" (1496; I'll have to tighten up on them! Bernarda: Remember that this is your obligation). Perhaps that is why she reminds her daughters that she has a set of chains for each of them and that she will use them if she has to do so. Whether Bernarda believes it or not, she finds it convenient to tell La Poncia "*Afortunadamente mis hijas me respetan y jamás torcieron mi voluntad*" (1500; Fortunately my daughters respect me and never went against my wishes). Her line is quite different to her daughters, whom she threatens, "*Ahora vigilaré sin cerrarlos [ojos] ya hasta que me muera*" (1503; Now I shall stay alert without ever closing [my eyes] until I die).

Bernarda does not miss an opportunity to let her daughters know her ideas on the loyalty that children owe to their parents and what the consequences are for not giving to their parents what is due to them. As the third act begins, Bernarda, her daughters, and their visitor Prudencia are finishing dinner. It is rare for Bernarda to have a guest in her home, and she welcomes this one to stay as long as possible, if for no other reason than to get some information out of her. Bernarda never knows what chance comment may give her a bit of gossip that she may be able to use to her advantage in the future.

Her duplicity, deceitfulness, and hypocrisy reach their depths in the final moments of the play. When she learns that Adela has hanged herself, Bernarda Alba seems unmoved by her daughter's death (she may even be relieved by it): "*Y no quiero llantos. La muerte hay que mirarla cara a cara*" (1532, And I do not want tears. Death must be faced squarely). What does concern her is that the town get the message that *"ella, la hija menor de Bernarda Alba, ha muerto virgen"* (1532; she, Bernarda Alba's youngest daughter, has died a virgin). Then the Maid announces that the neighbors have awaken; Bernarda will no longer be able to perpetuate the lie. Her power over the town is about to crumble. Bernarda's entire philosophy may be summed up in one comment she makes to Angustias: *"Quiero una buena fachada"* (1513; I want a good facade).

Of the five daughters, Adela has the greatest impact on the course of the play. She is the youngest (20 years old), the most attractive and spirited, and the most rebellious against the iron-fisted rule of her mother. It is she who from the start of the play to the finish causes Bernarda the greatest problems. Their conflict begins with the incident of the floral fan and ends with the final confrontation and then her suicide, which will continue to haunt her mother. The fan may well express Adela's connection with nature and her optimistic spirit. This major incident (there are no *minor* incidents in the play) sets the stage for the basic conflict of values and personalities that dominates the drama. Oddly enough, the next time Adela speaks it is to do harm to her eldest sister Angustias. Adela knows how her mother regards men and their conversation, which she considers unfit for her daughters' ears, so Adela tells Bernarda ("with intention") that she saw her sister listening to the men who were speaking about a subject of which Bernarda does not approve of her daughters hearing: a sexual scandal in town.

Almost immediately afterward, Adela puts on a green dress and goes out to the corral, calling to the chickens to notice her and somehow escaping Bernarda's watchful eye. It is hardly the chickens that concern Adela, and it would not have distressed her one bit if the attention that she received came from men rather than chickens. Adela is no fool, and she realizes that this eight-year period of mourning has come at the worst possible time for her. She is 20 years old and knows that by the time she reaches 28, she will no longer be the young, attractive woman that she is now; instead, she will have become another old maid sister in the family. What is worse, by her very nature Adela is not the kind of person who can stand being locked away from the world. She needs social interaction and, yes, men in her life.

The biggest blow she suffers is learning that Pepe el Romano, the most eligible bachelor around, is planning to marry her sister Angustias. She is dumbfounded at the news, which she learns secondhand from her sisters. She refuses to believe that he could be capable of such an act. She lashes out against the sisters around her. "*No me acostumbraré. Yo no puedo estar encerrada. No quiero que se me pongan las carnes como a vosotras; no quiero perder mi blancura en estas habitaciones; mañana me pondré mi vestido verde y me echaré a pasear por la calle. ¡Yo quiero salir!*" (1466; I won't get used to this. I can't be locked up. I don't want my skin to become like yours; I don't want to lose my vitality in these rooms; tomorrow I am going to put on my green dress and walk through the street. I want to get out!).

By the beginning of the second act, she is a topic of conversation for her sisters. She stays in bed all the time without any energy, and she is jumpy, " . . . *como si tuviese una lagartija entre los pechos*" (1472; . . . as if she had a lizard between her breasts). She is also starting to take on the look of a crazy woman. When finally she emerges from her room, her preoccupation is with her body, to which she makes several references. "*Tengo mal cuerpo*" (1478; My body doesn't feel well), and "*Yo hago con mi cuerpo lo que me parece*" (1479; I do whatever I want to with my body). So, too, her sister Martirio, who was supposed to have said to Adela (as the latter quotes her), "*¡Qué lástima de cuerpo que no vaya a ser para nadie!*" (1479; What a pity that her body will never belong to anyone!). Adela's response is that her body will go to anyone she wishes.

That anyone is Pepe el Romano. Apparently, she has already given her body to him. The housekeeper asks her, "*¿Por qué te pusiste casi desnuda con la luz encendida y la ventana abierta al pasar Pepe el segundo día que vino a hablar con tu hermana?*" (1480–81; Why did you show yourself almost naked with a light burning and the window open on the second day that Pepe came to speak to your sister?). La Poncia is ineffective in convincing Adela not to interfere in the proposed marriage between Pepe and Angustias, and in the following speech Adela shows how physical a person she is and how much she needs a man: "*Es inútil tu consejo. Ya es tarde. No por encima de ti, que eres una criada; por encima de mi madre saltaría para apagarme* *este fuego que tengo levantado por piernas y boca*" (1482; Your advice is useless. It's too late. Not just over you, a maid; but I would even jump over my mother to put out the fire that burns up from my legs to my mouth). There is a strong similarity between this statement and the speech that the Bride makes to the Mother at the end of *Blood Wedding*. Both women are controlled by their sexual desires. Pepe is Adela's source of strength. By looking into his eyes, she slowly drinks his blood into her. Nothing can now stop what has become inevitable.

Adela needs more than just a man, she needs freedom. Perhaps her greatest desire is to be able to walk freely in the country, breathe free air, even work in the fields, anything that will take her out of the confines of her house. She envies the migrant workers who have come to work in her region because they have the freedom to come and go. If she could come and go, she would be able to forget the problems that are consuming her.

Adela's conflict with her mother in the first act is over something as trivial as the color of a fan. Their confrontation in the second act is far more serious and personal. While Bernarda is calling for the death of the single woman who gave birth to and killed her baby, Adela is fighting for the woman's release. The last time she screams out against Bernarda, who wants hot coals inserted into the sinner's body, Adela grabs her belly and thereby gives the suggestion that she too may be with child.

By the third act, the tension has reached its peak: Angustias now wears the ring of pearls that Pepe has given her as a sign of their engagement, and Adela is forced to view the physical representation of her loss of Pepe. In Prudencia's presence, she predicts an unhappy future for her sister and insists that no one can foresee what the future may bring, thereby expressing her hope against hope that she may one day have Pepe for herself.

Adela is nervous. She comes to the dining room to drink water and goes to the doorway for fresh air. She claims that her thirst has woken her up. In her nightgown, she walks toward the corral and has her final confrontation with her sister Martirio (which will be further discussed later in this chapter). She again talks of the effect of Pepe on her life.

Characters

Ya no aguanto el horror de estos techos después de haber probado el sabor de su boca. Seré lo que el quiera que sea. Todo el pueblo contra mí, quemándome con sus dedos de lumbre, perseguida por los que dicen que son decentes, y me pondré la corona de espinas que tienen las que son queridas de algún hombre casado. (1528; I can no longer tolerate the horror of this roof after having tasted his mouth. I'll be whatever he wants of me. With the entire town against me, burning me with their illuminating fingers, pursued by those who call themselves decent, I'll wear the crown of thorns of those who are the lovers of a married man).

Adela is prepared to renounce all the decency of conventional society for the physical pleasure and emotional strength that she gets from that man. She will live alone in a shack where Pepe can find her when he needs her if that is the only way that she can share any time with him.

At the sound of Pepe's whistling, Adela runs toward the door. Martirio screams for Bernarda and shows her the signs of Adela's sin—the straw on the nightgown in which she lay with Pepe. In a moment of desperation and frustration, Adela commits the final act of rebellion against her mother: she breaks her mother's walking stick, the symbol of her authority, and thereby declares herself free of Bernarda's domination. *"Esto hago yo con la vara de la dominadora. No dé usted un paso más. En mí no manda más que Pepe"* (1529; This is what I do with the staff of the domineering woman. Don't come a step closer. Nobody except Pepe rules over me). Adela has declared herself free from her mother's domination, but her freedom is short-lived. At Martirio's suggestion that Bernarda has shot Pepe, Adela knows that she cannot continue to live with neither Pepe nor the possibility of escape from the oppressive house of Bernarda Alba, and she hangs herself.

Bernarda's presence may well dominate the play, but she is hardly a likely choice for the Lorquian heroine of the play; she is not a character for whom the audience feels pity or for whom the author feels sympathy. Not so in the case of Adela. She represents the ideals that Lorca admired—daring and unconventionality. She dares to take on society's mores and to act according to her own needs and beliefs. She lives for love and dies out of frustration. She suffers oppression; only with Pepe or in death could she be free. When she believes that she can no longer have Pepe, she has to resign herself to the only other chance of escape that she sees—death.

The housekeeper's role may be the most complex in the play. She is all things to all characters in the play without ever being a hypocrite and is therefore a character worthy of admiration. She has the insight and earthy wisdom of her predecessor, the Maid in *Blood Wedding*. Like Adela's, La Poncia's life is one of frustration because of her resentment of Bernarda. In the opening scene of the play, when she is alone with the Maid, she is able to express herself freely. La Poncia has been in Bernarda's employ for 30 years of

> *lavando sus sábanas . . . comiendo sus sobras; noches en vela cuando tose; días enteros mirando por la rendija para espiar a los vecinos y llevarle el cuento; vida sin secretos una con otra. . . . Pero soy una buena perra; ladro cuando me lo dicen y muerdo los talones de los que piden limosna cuando ella me azuza.* (1442; washing her sheets . . . eating her leftovers; awake nights when she coughs; whole days of watching through the window to spy on the neighbors and bring her the news; a life without secrets from each other. . . . But I am a good dog; I bark when they tell me to and bite the heels of the beggars when she tells me to sick them).

La Poncia is torn between debt to and hate of the woman who is "*capaz de sentarse encima de tu corazón y ver como te mueres durante un año sin que se le cierre esa sonrisa fría que lleva en su maldita cara*" (1441; capable of sitting on your heart and watching you die for a year without ever losing the frozen smile on her damned face). La Poncia's debt to Bernarda is a financial one: not only does Bernarda employ her, but both of the housekeeper's married sons work Bernarda's land. Bernarda controls the financial fate of the entire family.

Her indebtness to Bernarda does not prevent her from being frank with her employer; Lorca gave her that right as a privilege of age. In the list of characters, the playwright specified the age of each one; he made Bernarda and La Poncia exactly the same age—60 years old—

and thereby made them equals. La Poncia has the right to speak freely to Bernarda, and so she does right from the start of the play. When Bernarda orders the mourners out of her house, for example, the housekeeper reminds her that she can have no complaints because the entire town attended the funeral.

La Poncia acts as a mediator between Bernarda and her daughters and is clearly on the side of the underdogs. She stops Bernarda from beating Angustias for listening to the men's conversation and tries to calm the mother's rage. She gives to the daughters something they do not receive from their mother: friendly and earthy conversation, a pleasant and light note to their lives. For example, she tells of when her late husband first came to court her, of how nervous both of them were, and of how she punished him when he did not act properly. She also gives the daughters some practical ideas of what marriage is really like: "*A los quince días de boda, deja la cama por la mesa y luego la mesa por la tabernilla, y la que no se conforma se pudre llorando en un rincón*" (1476; After the first two weeks of marriage, he [a husband] leaves the bed for the table and then the table for the tavern, and the woman who does not get used to it ends up rotting away in the corner). La Poncia is no one's fool: when she had to hit her husband once in a while, she did.

In addition to being a friend to the daughters, she is also their conscience. For example, she is aware of Adela's sexual relationship with Pepe, and she threatens to expose the secret if Adela does not end it immediately. When her threats do not work, she tries to use reason, to give encouragement:

> *No seas como los niños chicos. ¡Deja en paz a tu hermana, y si Pepe el Romano te gusta, te aguantas! (ADELA llora.) Además, ¿quién dice que no te puedes casar con él? Tu hermana Angustias es una enferma. Esa no resiste el primer parto. Es estrecha de cintura, vieja, y con mi conocimiento te digo que se morirá. Entonces Pepe hará lo que hacen todos los viudos de esta tierra: se casará con la más joven, la más hermosa, y esa serás tú* (1481; Don't act like a little child. Leave your sister in peace, and if you like Pepe, you have to put up with the situation! (ADELA cries.) Besides, who

says that you can't marry him? Your sister Angustias is sickly. She
will not make it through the first childbirth. She has a narrow waist,
is old, according to my understanding I tell you that she will die.
Then Pepe will do what all of the widowers of this land do: he will
marry the youngest, prettiest woman, and that will be you).

Her words have no effect on Adela, who wants the old woman to
mind her own business and do her work. Whatever Adela's attitude,
La Poncia will be her shadow. La Poncia's motives are as selfish as
they are altruistic. She is an elderly woman, and she wants to live in a
respectable house, not one at which the neighbors spit in disgust as
they pass.

In each act, La Poncia has a frank conversation with Bernarda.
The first time is after Bernarda's beating of Angustias. When Bernarda
orders everyone out of the room, La Poncia knows that she is not
included in the command; she has special privileges and may even
know intuitively that Bernarda wants to speak to her. Bernarda uses
the occasion to gather gossip against Paca la Roseta, a married woman
who is involved in a sexual scandal. La Poncia uses the occasion to
speak up on behalf of the daughters. She thinks that they are too good,
that they do not give Bernarda enough trouble. She tries to make Bernarda realize that she is not doing right by her daughters; that it is
time for Angustias to marry; that if the social class of the men in the
town is below what Bernarda considers her own to be, then she has
to move to another town, even if she is not the richest woman in the
new place. When the conversation takes on a tone that does not please
Bernarda, she ends it by reminding La Poncia that she has no right to
be speaking intimately with her employer and that it is her job to
serve.

And yet the conversations between the two older women persist,
each at a more intimate level than the last. The second conversation
is after the incident of Angustias's photograph of Pepe showing up
between the sheets of Martirio's bed. Both servant and employer begin
by agreeing that Angustias's wedding to Pepe should take place as
soon as possible, both to get Angustias out of the house and to get

Pepe away from it. La Poncia can now begin to bring up the message that she needs to convey to Bernarda. She tries to let her know that there are big problems in the house that Bernarda refuses to see and that they will only get worse if she does not lighten up on her daughters. Bernarda once again does not like the direction that the conversation is taking, so she throws in La Poncia's face how her mother died in the poorhouse.

And yet La Poncia persists. Pepe should not be marrying Angustias; he should be marrying Adela, who is really his girlfriend. Pepe does not belong with Angustias, it is just not a natural match. As the conversation deteriorates into a verbal battle, La Poncia uses her strongest ammunition against Bernarda; she lets her know that there is talk about her house around town. La Poncia is the bridge between Bernarda's house and the outside world. La Poncia's son reports that Pepe was still around the house at 4 A.M. Bernarda is determined to keep a ceaseless vigil on the house for as long as she lives.

In the third act, again, they talk at a moment when Bernarda is enjoying a false sense of security. Pepe is supposed to be out of town and not coming for a visit that night; Bernarda thinks that she will have a peaceful evening and a good night's sleep. Either in an attempt to gloat over La Poncia who had been predicting big problems ahead for Bernarda's family, or to gloat over the absence of talk in the town about the household, Bernarda insists that the crisis that La Poncia predicted has not occurred and will not. La Poncia is willing to acknowledge that on the outside the daughters may seem to be living normally, but she insists that it takes only a look into their hearts to observe the true depth of their unhappiness. La Poncia also lets Bernarda know that she keeps more information under her hat than Bernarda can imagine, but that at any moment "lightning may strike" in the form of tragedy.

In the opening conversation of the play, before Bernarda returns from the funeral, La Poncia tells the Maid that one day she will finally become completely fed up and on that day she will lock herself in a room for an entire year with Bernarda, spitting on her employer, "*Bernarda, por esto, por aquello, por lo otro*" (1442; Bernarda, for this, for that, for the other thing). In her last conversation with the Maid in the third act, La Poncia does not mind revealing Adela's secret, which previously she had kept to herself. She shows, too, her astute abilities as a judge of human character in her analysis of Martirio (which appears later in this chapter).

The most difficult task that she takes upon herself is to make peace between Adela and Martirio, the one she refers to as the worst of the daughters, "a poisoned well." Martirio is a more important character than Angustias (who is ostensibly responsible for Pepe's presence around the house) because it is Martirio who is really the thorn in Adela's side, and Adela is probably the tragic heroine of the play. Martirio is constantly watching Adela, even when Adela is asleep; she follows Adela around as if she were her sister's shadow. Martirio is motivated less by sisterly love than by jealousy. She, too, is in love with Pepe. Of the five sisters, Martirio, at the age of 24 (second youngest), is the least likely candidate for marriage. She does not have Angustias's money, Adela's looks, Magdalena's humanity, or Amelia's ingenuity. She is a physically pathetic sight: weak, ugly, and hunchbacked. She states that she has always been afraid of men and hated the thought of having to grow up and be embraced by one of them. She thanks the good Lord for having made her so unattractive. She did have a boyfriend once, Enrique Humanas, but her mother put an end to that relationship before it had a chance to blossom.

Her personality is no better than her looks. She behaves more like a robot than a human being, with no faith in anything, including herself. She cares little if she lives or dies and takes the medicine prescribed for her more out of routine than out of concern for her health. In addition, she is a hypocrite. She claims that having or not having a boyfriend is all the same to her, but such is not the case. She is consumed by both sexual frustration and jealousy of Angustias, who will have Pepe legally, and Adela, who has him physically. Her desperation leads her to steal Angustias's photograph of Pepe; if she cannot have the man, she will settle for his likeness. Martirio is a younger version of her mother. In the scene of the unmarried mother, she concurs with Bernarda that the woman should be killed. In addition, it is she who leads Adela to believe that Bernarda has killed Pepe and thereby brings about her sister's suicide.

Hypocrisy becomes mixed with hate, resentment, and jealousy in her confrontation with Adela in the third act. She follows Adela to the corral, where her younger sister has her rendezvous with Pepe, but her motives for doing so are confused and confusing. Does she enjoy just the thought of knowing where she can find Pepe, the chance of getting a glimpse of him, the voyeuristic pleasure of seeing Adela with him, or the possibility of keeping Adela from having him? Or is it true when she says that she does not want to live in a house where such evil deeds are taking place and ruining the good name of her family?

Her moment of defeat occurs when Adela forces her to admit that she loves Pepe, but that Pepe loves Adela. *"Clávame un cuchillo si es tu gusto, pero no me lo digas más"* (1527; Stick a knife into me if you want to, but don't tell me again [that he loves you]). At that moment, Adela feels genuine pity or perhaps affection for her sister and tries to embrace her, but Martirio rebuffs her sister's overtures. They are no longer kin; she can no longer see Adela as a sister, only as another woman.

The other sisters are pale in contrast with Adela and Martirio and are secondary characters in the play. However, each has her own distinctive personality, and the reader must be careful not to treat them as an undistinguished mass. Angustias is only a half-sister to the other four, since she was the fruit of Bernarda's first marriage. It is she alone of all the sisters who has an inheritance worth mentioning—which is why she has Pepe for a fiancé. Angustias is not much more physically appealing than Martirio. She is 39 years old, sickly, and nasal. Bernarda wants Angustias to forgive Martirio for the incident about Pepe's picture. Whether or not Bernarda believes Martirio's claim that she took it as a joke on her sister, Bernarda does use that reason with Angustias. They are sisters and must put on the appearance of getting along together.

Magdalena (30 years old) and Amelia (27 years old) play the least important roles of all the sisters. Magdalena was the most devoted daughter to her father and it is she who faints during the funeral mass.

She alone of the household truly misses him. She is as realistic as she is pessimistic; she knows that she is never going to get married and, like Martirio, claims not to care if she lives or dies. She does seem to feel compassion for Adela's plight and would be willing to make a sacrifice to see her happy. Like Adela, she is sick at the thought of having to spend the next eight years in a dark house. She curses her lot at having been born a woman and nostalgically longs for the good old days, which she remembers as a happy period in her life. She knows hypocrisy when she hears it and speaks out against it, such as when Martirio is guilty of it, and similarly, when Amelia is. She does have a confrontation with Angustias when she expresses her doubt that Angustias will actually marry and get out of the house. Ahead of her time, she believes that women should be strong and forceful and should not tolerate shabby treatment from men, including husbands. As does La Poncia, Magdalena recognizes that Martirio is "possessed." She feels both jealousy and selfishness toward Angustias; when La Poncia suggests that the sisters make clothes for the christening of Angustias's future first child, Magdalena alone refuses to contribute a stitch to the project. After Adela breaks her mother's stick and runs after Pepe, Magdalena expresses the wish that Adela would get out so that the family would never have to see her again. In a manner of speaking, she gets her wish.

Amelia is the least striking of the sisters, and the hardest character for students of the play to remember. She is a kind-hearted person who hates to hear her mother speak unkindly of the neighbors and who is concerned about Martirio's health (even if Martirio is not). She worries about Magdalena tripping from an open shoelace, which does not bother Magdalena very much. Like Martirio, Amelia feels unsure of herself around men and would die of embarrassment if she ever had to hear a proposal of marriage, as Angustias heard from Pepe. Like Magdalena, who curses womankind, Amelia believes that being born a woman is life's worst punishment. She also seems to be afraid of almost everything, from the horse in the corral to a shooting star. Unlike Adela, who likes to bring light to subjects that have for too long been kept in the dark (she likes the truth, just as her grandmother does), Amelia closes her eyes so that she will not have to see what is going on in the world.

María Josefa, Bernarda's octogenarian mother, is the most truthful and poetic character in the play and the one most closely identified with Adela. They share the common desire of wanting to get out and be free. María Josefa has good reason for wanting to get out: her heartless daughter keeps her locked up, out of sight and out of mind. María Josefa is the voice of truth, and truth is a painful concept for Bernarda. It is through the character of María Josefa that the reader sees that Bernarda does not discriminate against anyone: she is as mean to her mother as she is to her daughters, neighbors, and servants. Bernarda keeps her locked up not so much to keep her safe from harming herself as to keep her out of the view of the townspeople. What might they think of the rest of the family if they saw Bernarda's "crazy" mother?

It is true that what she wants is out of the realm of reason. At the age of 80, she wants to get married to a virile man and have lots of children. Like Yerma, she wants to participate in the process of life. Her confrontation with Bernarda brings the first act to an end. "*Me escapé porque me quiero casar, porque quiero casarme con un varón hermoso de la orilla del mar, ya que aquí los hombres huyen de las mujeres*" (1470; I escaped because I want to get married, because I want to marry a handsome man from the seashore, since the men from around here run away from women). She is more aware than her daughter of the situation in the household and will not be a part of it. "*No quiero ver a estas mujeres solteras rabiando por la boda, haciéndose polvo el corazón, y yo me quiero ir a mi pueblo. Bernarda, yo quiero un varón para casarme y para tener alegría*" (1470; I don't want to see these old maids seething for marriage, withering and heartbroken, and I want to go to my own town. Bernarda, I want a man to marry and be happy). She also refuses to leave any of her possessions behind her; she will give nothing to her old maid granddaughters who will never marry. Her reason for wanting to marry is much like Yerma's for wanting to have a child: both want to be a part of the fertile world around them. In her second and final appearance on stage, she tells Martirio, "*Yo quiero campo. Yo quiero casas, pero casas abiertas y las vecinas acostadas en sus camas con sus niños chiquitos y los hombres fuera sentados en sus sillas*" (1525; I want the countryside. I want houses, but open houses and neighbors, the women sleeping in bed with their little children and the men sitting outside in their chairs).

She also has the keenest insight of any of the characters into Pepe el Romano, whom she refers to as a giant loved by every one of the sisters. She knows, too, that he will devour them. In this second appearance, she is carrying a lamb in her arms and singing a lullaby to it. She knows that it is not a real baby, but that it is better than nothing, which is what her granddaughters have. Much of the vocabulary in María Josefa's speeches is fraught with imagery (which will be discussed in Chapter 7).

Not a single man appears on stage in this play, although the presence of men is pervasive. Pepe and the other men will be treated not as characters but as part of the play's themes and images in the next two chapters.

chapter 6

Themes

The structure, plot, and characters all serve to embody a theme or series of themes in a play. This chapter will examine the themes of the three plays both as they explain the individual works and as they make a trilogy of the three plays. The plays in Lorca's trilogy are all concerned with the problems or frustrations of women: love, sex, motherhood, marriage, and lack of freedom. They underscore how little control the individual has in achieving personal satisfaction and in determining the course of her own life. To one degree or another, all the women in the trilogy (with the exception of a minor character here and there) suffer in their own personal hells.

All the women in *Blood Wedding* have good reasons to be frustrated and unhappy. The Mother has had a life filled with misery and suffering. She has witnessed the death of her husband and older son. Her only hope for happiness is her one remaining son, the Bridegroom; he is her only living relative, the only chance for her to have grandchildren and to see the continuity of the family line. She has never gotten over the pain caused by her losses, nor has she been able to stop hating the Félix clan, which is responsible for the tragedies in her life. It is understandable that she be concerned about the woman her son is about to marry. She worries about his future happiness, the good name of her family, and posterity. Typical of the women in Lorca's plays, her worst fears turn into reality. The Bride once had a boyfriend whom she has never been able to get out of her emotional system. The Bride does in fact run off with her former boyfriend on the night of her wedding to the Bridegroom. In the duel to win back his wife, the Bridegroom is killed. The Mother thereby loses her only remaining son and sole living relative. She is partially the cause of his death, since it was she who insisted that he pursue the Bride after the flight with Leonardo. Her pain, resentment, and frustration are locked into her life in the physical presence of the Bride, who now shares her home.

The Bride's tragedy in life is self-induced but tragic nonetheless. She is a woman controlled by her irresistible attraction to Leonardo, an attraction that even marriage does not diminish. It is this impulse (which she describes so provocatively in the quotation in the previous chapter) that determines the course of her life: she is the helpless victim of her sexual attraction to a man she cannot have. He is married, she is married; their escape together can only end in tragedy. The cause of her tragedy is that, through no fault of her own, she could not marry the man nature had intended for her. He married the respectable and dependable, if unexciting and less sensual, woman who would be the mother of his children.

Leonardo's wife's life is one of quiet desperation. She is no fool and can see that she is hardly her husband's first concern; she ranks somewhat lower than the son she produced for him, and certainly lower than his mysterious ventures away from home. Even the day of the Bride's marriage, which has the potential of returning her husband to her, is a painful day for the Wife. Leonardo refuses to accompany her to the wedding in the carriage and instead travels alone by horse. It is the moment when she finally announces that she cannot stand anymore; Leonardo echoes her sentiments. She sees her husband looking at her with thorns of hate in his eyes—or rather, resentment, resentment of her and their relationship, which keep him from spending his life with the woman he really loves. The Wife suffers the public humiliation of having to announce that her husband has just run off with the Bride.

Two other minor characters in the play also suffer on account of Leonardo's relationship with the Bride. The first is his mother-in-law. A typical grandmother, she lavishes attention and affection on the baby in her arms. When she notices that Leonardo's horse is worn out and looks as if it had just returned from the other end of the earth, she knows intuitively that something is wrong and can only hope that there will be no consequences for her daughter or grandson. The last character of any substance is the Bride's maid. As noted in the previous chapter, the Maid is a perceptive woman and concerned enough about her employer to detect that she is having problems and needs advice. The Bride's problems are also hers; when the Bride suffers, so does she. Even Leonardo is frustrated, but his problem is of his own making: he decided before the play begins to abandon the Bride and marry another, more acceptable woman than she is.

The most notable example of anguish is Yerma's, whose suffering is largely out of her hands. Unlike the Bride, who brings about her own tragedy through her act of running away with Leonardo, only part of Yerma's struggle is her own; the other part is up to her husband. She wishes that she could have children alone, but, alas, her wish runs counter to the laws of biology. In the personage of Yerma, character, theme, and imagery are all perfectly interwoven: her name in Spanish means a barren woman, which is also her personal struggle and the theme of the play. She is perhaps the most lamentable example of frustration: she is driven by the dual preoccupations of wanting to become a mother and trying to understand the reason for her barren state. There is no escape from her plight.

If Yerma is frustrated because she cannot have children, participate in the process of life, and serve a function in her society, the Second Girl is frustrated because she has all that Yerma desires. Her problem is that participation in the traditional role of Spanish womanhood is forced upon her by her mother; the young woman would prefer to be single, live with her former boyfriend, and not have to become a mother or keep house. She is bound by the role that society has prescribed for her and will never be at liberty to alter her status in life.

Just in case readers and audiences failed to notice that the first two plays are about the plight of Spanish women, the third bears the subtitle "Drama about Women in the Towns of Spain." *The House of Bernarda Alba* has more frustrated women than any other play that Lorca ever wrote, maybe more than any play by any author in modern dramatic literature. At the top of the list is Adela. There is little doubt that her dilemma was Lorca's central concern. She is the most pitiable character in the play because she has more to lose than any other. She is young, pretty, and hopeful. She has her whole life in front of her and wants it filled with the two things that she needs most in life, men and freedom. Her optimism is irrational and faulty for a variety of reasons. First of all, she can see that her tyrannical mother keeps her and her sisters at an unhealthy distance from men. Secondly, she should realize that her affair with her sister's fiancé can only lead to problems. Finally, she would have to be blind to the society all around her not to know that men and freedom are mutually exclusive possibilities for a Spanish woman. Like the Bride, Adela's frustration is the consequence of wanting a man she just cannot have because he already belongs to another woman. Also like the Bride, she cannot deny what her hormones experience when she is in the presence of the man she loves; his power over her is undeniable. Despite Martirio's belief that Adela's problem is no different from her sisters', it is Adela alone who acts upon her desires and tries to satisfy them and escape from the hellish household of Bernarda Alba. She is, after all, a granddaughter of María Josefa.

The other sisters are resigned to their fate and lack the faith that Adela has that she can control the course of her life. The causes of Angustias's unhappiness are several. She does not feel comfortable with the man she is about to marry. She knows that he keeps secrets from her and that even when they are together his thoughts are far away and not on her. In addition, she must live with the knowledge that Pepe is marrying her not for herself but for her money. She also knows that her own sister is sexually involved with her husband-to-be. Martirio may be the most frustrated of all the sisters. She is consumed by her desire to have Pepe but has nothing to attract him. Still a young woman in her own mind, María Josefa also suffers in the frustration that is pervasive in Bernarda Alba's house. She needs to be free, and even if her hopes of marrying a virile young man and having lots of children are out of touch with reality, her desire to get out of her daughter's house and control is real. Like the Mother in *Blood Wedding*, María Josefa is witnessing the end of her line and suffers at the thought that her granddaughters will never marry, have children, and be happy.

Also within the household are La Poncia and the Maid. La Poncia lives in constant resentment of her employer and with the knowledge that whenever it suits her purposes Bernarda will once again bring up La Poncia's past and show disrespect for her dead mother. There is no escape for her, just as there is no escape for Bernarda's daughters or aged mother; she is bound to Bernarda's house by economic necessity. So is the Maid, whose life is nothing more than cleaning the house until her hands bleed but never meeting with Bernarda's approval.

Bernarda's influence extends beyond her own home: she controls and frustrates the lives of all her neighbors. She knows their secrets, and so they live in fear of the emotional blackmail that she uses to keep them in their place. The neighbor Prudencia's frustration is caused by her husband, who refuses to forgive their daughter for an incident that took place long in the past. And Adelaida (a character who never appears on stage and is discussed later in this chapter) knows that her past determines her future, that women in Spain are caught in the web of a male-dominated society, which protects men and punishes women. Her mother suffered at the hands of men, and so does she. While Bernarda is the cause of so much suffering, she is also her own victim. The price of the control she wishes to maintain is constant vigilance and denial to herself of the same freedom that she denies to those around her.

Why did Lorca write these plays? In large measure, they are informed by his sense of social justice. Already in his poetry he had championed the causes of persecuted minorities, for example, gypsies and blacks. He wanted to call attention to the plight of women in his native land. He wanted to show that the repression or frustration of the natural desires for love, sex, and motherhood in accordance with society's norms can have tragic consequences. While it is not likely that Lorca would have wanted to convey the message that a sexual relationship leads to death (as Adela's does), the message is certainly contained in *The House of Bernarda Alba;* that message is even more meaningful in the current age of AIDS than it was when Lorca wrote the play. But Lorca's plays contain more than a lament for his characters; they also have a warning for society at large about the tragic cost of repressing any of its members.

It is not just thwarted love and sexual frustration that cause the suffering of Lorca's characters, especially the women; there are a host of other social and personal ideals and conflicts. There are underlying causes for the sexual and affectional problems of mismatched pairs. First of all, there is the traditional woman's role in Spain's rigidly structured society. Throughout the plays, characters spout lines that reflect the ideas that have kept women from achieving freedom and equality in Spain. The characters who express those ideas are sometimes the men who keep women suppressed; at other times such ideas are voiced by the women who have internalized the messages that they have seen and heard throughout their lives.[1] The first character in the three plays to express such a sentiment is the Mother in *Blood Wedding.* She tells her son of how his grandfather was a real man, one who left a child in every corner of the region. That is what the Mother likes—men who are real men. In the same conversation, she expresses herself on women: they should be modest and hard-working, they should knead dough and sew clothes. It is this definition of the traditional roles of men and women that keeps Yerma in a spiritual frenzy and Bernarda's daughters in an emotional prison. In the song that the Maid sings as she does her work in the opening moments of the second scene of act 2 of *Blood Wedding,* one line is about a woman never leaving the house again after her wedding.

Perhaps the worst tradition determining the course of women's lives is their lack of choice over their own mates. The marriages are arranged for them by their fathers, as was Yerma's. How she describes her life to Juan serves as her definition of marriage and of the role of women in relation to men. "*Vivo submisa a ti, y lo que sufro lo guardo pegado a mis carnes. Y cada día que pase será peor*" (1313; I live subservient to you, and whatever I suffer I keep close to my own skin. And every day that passes it will get worse). She tries to make Juan understand that unlike men, who have their work and social life, all that women have is the job of raising children; without that job, they have no reason for living. Víctor's definition of life shows that he too is bound by tradition, but his definition does not include a role for women: "*La acequia por su sitio, el rebaño en el redil, la luna en el cielo y el hombre con su arado*" (1323; The acacia tree in its place, the flock of sheep in the fold, the moon in the sky, and man with his plow). In *Yerma*, the conflict between husband and wife is not only about the problem of having and not having children—a fate that they cannot control—but about the proper conduct for a married woman. For Juan, there is almost nothing proper for his wife to do except remain at home; that is the only sure way of keeping his name off the tongues of the townspeople. He berates his wife for speaking to Víctor in public out of the fear not so much of what they might do together as of what people might think and say about his wife or about him. And he is correct in his suspicions. In the next scene, the Washer-women are commenting on Yerma's behavior in public: they know how painful it is for her to stay at home and that she sits outside alone at night. Juan is just not satisfied with the way Yerma acts. He has his belief of "*las ovejas en el redil y las mujeres en su casa*" (1312; sheep in the fold and women in the house), but Yerma is not able to accept his traditional beliefs. What Yerma needs is someone to keep her at home—a child; if she had one and could fit into society, she would not have to transgress its norms. But she does not have a child, and that lack forms her attitudes. Yerma wants to be a part of nature, but Juan knows that she is not going to see flowers by walking around at night: she is going to see men, and that is not good for either of them. Her conduct can do nothing but place his honor in jeopardy; whether the suspicions of the town are well-founded or not, the neighbors still point at Juan when they see him on the street.

Traditions are the foundation on which Bernarda runs her own and the lives of her daughters. The first law that she lays down in *The House of Bernarda Alba* is that the household will mourn her late husband for eight years, because that is how things were in her father's and her grandfather's homes. Nothing must change. And the daughters will do what is proper for them, which is to sit and embroider their trousseaux. When Magdalena objects to having to sit in the house day after day (she would prefer even heavy labor), Bernarda reminds her, "*Eso tiene ser mujer*" (1452; That's what being a woman is all about). Magdalena curses womanhood if that is what it is all about. For Bernarda, it is all quite simple: "*Hilo y aguja para las hembras. Látigo y mula para el varón*" (1452; Thread and a needle for women. A whip and a mule for a man). It is tradition and Bernarda's interpretation and enforcement of it that ruin the lives of her daughters. Their biggest problem is their lack of any kind of freedom, including the freedom just to get out of the house, to take a walk in the country, to breathe fresh air. Magdalena believes that women are so dependent upon men that not even their own eyes belong to them.

There are several interrelated themes in the trilogy, such as honor and gossip, and status and land and money. The theme of honor appears in all three plays. The Mother in *Blood Wedding* introduces the subject during her meeting with the Father of the Bride. Her source of pride is that her son has "*la honra más limpia que una sábana puesta al sol*" (1198; cleaner honor than a bedsheet drying in the sun). It is for her son's honor that she insists that he chase after Leonardo and the Bride, thereby bringing about his death. In the Spanish system of values, life without honor is no life at all. Honor is also the subject of the Mother's final confrontation with the Bride, who insists that she is as honorable as a newborn baby.

While Yerma's burden is her barren state, at the heart of Juan's problem with his wife is the conflict between her sense of honor or personal dignity (*honra*) and his sense of social honor or reputation (*honor*). For Yerma, indulging in the sexual act solely for her or her husband's pleasure would go against her sense of *honra*. The act is justifiable to her only as a means to an end, and that end must be having a child. But the Washerwomen do not believe that Yerma has honor anyway because she allows herself to become the object of gossip. Juan feels compromised if Yerma goes as far as the fountain to get water for the dinner table. He accuses his sisters of not protecting the honor of the family's name by allowing Yerma out of the house. He also reminds his wife that "*las familias tienen honra y la honra es una carga que se lleva entre todos*" (1315; families have honor, and honor is the obligation that all must bear). Yerma is aware that she is living in a situation of three against one and that Juan and his sisters do not trust her, but she insists that "*lo primero de mi casta es la honradez*" (1319; the first value in my breeding is honor). It is understandable that when Juan finds Yerma with Dolores he should explode and ask where the honor of his house has gone. Yerma is offended that Juan thinks that only he and his family are people of honor and that honor is something unknown to her side. It is finally Yerma's sense of honor that keeps her from attempting to become pregnant by the son of the Old Woman. A child is worth a good deal to Yerma, but she draws the line when the price of the child would be her honor.

The themes of honor, reputation, gossip, and social position reach their height in *Bernarda Alba*. Here is a family that lives in fear of what the neighbors will say, and Bernarda has only herself to blame for the situation because she uses the technique of gathering gossip about her neighbors to manipulate them. She has hardly set foot onstage before she demonstrates her methods. A young girl who comes to her house innocently mentions that Pepe el Romano was at the funeral. It does not serve Bernarda's purposes to have his name come up, so she turns the situation into an attack on the decency of the Girl's family. She proclaims that the person everyone at the funeral saw was a widower who was very close to the Girl's aunt. The women know Bernarda and what she is doing and express to each other in stage whispers what a vicious person she is.

Amelia observes to Martirio that Adelaida was not at the wake, but Martirio is not surprised. Bernarda is the only person in town who knows the whole story about Adelaida's past, and she throws it in Adelaida's face every chance she gets. Adelaida is afraid of Bernarda and does not want to put herself in the position of hearing again about how her father killed the man who was then the husband of the woman he made his first wife; how he later abandoned his wife and went off with another woman, who then had a daughter with whom he entered into relations (Adelaida's mother); and finally how he married Adelaida's mother after driving his second wife to madness and death. Much of the gossip that Bernarda keeps filed in her head is of a sexual nature; some is about the background of the families, or about how they came into possession of their lands. Bernarda's first conversation with La Poncia reveals that it is the housekeeper's job to find out what is going on in town and to keep Bernarda informed.

As Magdalena puts it, the sisters are rotting away in dread of becoming the objects of gossip, which Bernarda calls "*el veneno más amargo que una madre puede resistir*" (1492; the most bitter poison that a mother has to endure). La Poncia knows the women of the town because she is one of them; she warns Bernarda that they can read minds and know when something is going on in someone else's home. The clue that Bernarda has lost her power over the neighbors is in the Maid's last line of the play, "*¡Se han levantado los vecinos!*" (1531; The neighbors have awakened!). They have awakened not just physically but also emotionally: Bernarda will no longer control them by talking of what goes on in their homes. There is now a scandal in Bernarda's house that evens out the score. Lie as she may, she will not be able to stop the talk about Adela hanging herself—or about her reasons for doing so.

Bernarda claims that her insistence on decency derives from the fact that she has a certain social position to maintain in the town; she and her daughters must set the example for everyone else. As Bernarda tells it, her social position is what keeps her daughters from getting married: Bernarda has a financial status that no one else in the town can equal. She will not allow her daughters to compromise themselves—or her status—by marrying beneath themselves. Bernarda is apparently quite satisfied with the situation just as it is, and she will not give up the social airs she puts on around town.

Money is another theme that binds the three plays to each other. Money does not make its first appearance in *Bernarda Alba*, where social pretensions have their most devastating effect; it appears in *Blood Wedding* and continues through *Yerma*. In the three plays, the source of wealth is the land. In fact, Lorca called these plays a "*trilogía dramática de la tierra española*" (1724; dramatic trilogy of the Spanish land). The Mother in *Blood Wedding* tells her neighbor that her son has been able to buy a vineyard as a result of his good fortune—and no doubt his hard work. His financial success is well known. The Young Woman comments to Leonardo's mother-in-law that the Bridegroom was at the store buying gifts for his bride-to-be and that everything was of the finest quality. The talk between the Mother and the Bride's father centers on amassing land. The Father observes, "*Tú eres más rica que yo. Las viñas valen un capital. Cada pámpano una moneda de plata*" (1196; You are richer than I am. The vineyards are capital. Each vine leaf is a silver coin). His wish is to be able to buy the land in between his and the Mother's and to have their children control all of it.

Juan also makes his money from the land. The money and the land dominate his life. According to Yerma, he spends his days with his sheep and his nights counting his money. He sums up the reasons for his success in life in one line: "*Las cosas de la labor van bien, no tenemos hijos que gasten*" (1275; My labors are going well, and we don't have children who spend money). Yerma can never have a child because Juan does not want one; it would upset his financial plan. What gets Víctor out of the picture is Juan's purchase of his flock which leaves Víctor free to move where his father wants him—and gets him away from Yerma.

Money controls the fate of Bernarda's daughters. Pepe does not decide to marry Angustias because she is the eldest and ugliest daughter but because she is the richest. Not only do Adela and Magdalena know why he is marrying her, but so does Angustias, who tells her sisters that an ounce of gold is worth more than physical beauty. Magdalena has to agree that money is all-powerful. The problem in Prudencia's family is also over money—again, an inheritance.

Aside from being a source of wealth, the land (and people of the land) exists as its own theme. In each of the three acts of *Blood Wed-*

ding, the subject comes up in three different contexts. The subject of the land first comes up when the Mother and the Bridegroom are on their way to meet the Bride and her father. The Bridegroom points out that the Bride's family owns good land. For the Mother, that parcel of land is too lonely; in four hours of travel, they have seen hardly a tree. She associates the loneliness of the landscape with the absence of a husband and older son in her life. The land bereft of trees reminds her of what her husband was able to do with his land. In the three years that he was married to the Mother, he planted ten cherry trees, developed a vineyard, and cultivated flowers. He made the earth flourish; he brought life to the land, as he brought forth sons and gave her joy. She knows that land in and of itself has no value until it is cultivated. In the second act, the Father speaks of his eagerness for the arrival of grandchildren because strong arms are needed to fight the constant battle of the land. And the workers should not be hired hands; they must be the owners of the land who have a stake in its future and productivity. In the third act, the subject of the land comes up in the conversation among the Woodcutters. They speak of the land drinking up blood. The last reference is in the final scene of the play: the Mother knows that she must face up to her tragedy, that she is left alone with her pain, her tears, and her land.

Each reference to the land corresponds to the situation in that segment of the play. The first reference is in the context of the Bride and her circumstances; the second is in the context of the marriage, which has the potential for bringing forth grandchildren; the third is in the foreshadowing of the deaths and the blood that they spill on the earth; finally, land is the only company the Mother will know for the rest of her life.

There is a distinct difference between Yerma's and Juan's relation to the land. Yerma tries to absorb its procreative powers; Juan wants only its wealth. Yerma thinks that she is a victim of her upbringing in the country. "*Las muchachas que se crían en el campo, como yo, tienen cerradas todas las puertas*" (1291; The girls who are brought up in the country, like I was, have all of the doors [in life] closed to them).

For the daughters of Bernarda Alba, the countryside is a source of refreshment and escape. They see the men who work the land as free and independent, as having everything that the women who are prisoners in the house do not have. (There will be a further development of this aspect of the play in Chapter 7.)

Another theme common to the three plays is that of family/blood/heredity. In *Blood Wedding,* the characters are divided into those of good and bad seed. The Mother and her husband are of good seed—hard workers, productive. Her father showed how strong a seed he had by leaving children in every corner of the region. On the other hand, Leonardo is of bad seed; nobody in his family has ever been any good, starting with his great-grandfather who was a killer and continuing up to the present generation. The contrast in the lineage of the two families, the good and bad blood, makes for "bad blood" between them. Although Leonardo was only eight years old when the Mother's husband and son were murdered, she knows that the blood of the Félix clan is in his veins. Leonardo even calls himself a "man of blood." He does not define the term, but in the context, he is suggesting that nobody insults him without risking being killed by him. The Bride's father agrees with the Mother's assessment of Leonardo. "*Ese busca la desgracia. No tiene buena sangre*" (1227; That man is looking for trouble. He does not have good blood). During the conversation about the marriage arrangements, the Mother assures the Bride's father that "*mi hijo la cubrirá bien. Es de buena simienta. Su padre pudo haber tenido conmigo muchos hijos*" (1228; my son will cover her well. He is of good seed. His father could have had many children with me). The Mother feels the familial bonds through blood. She was not afraid to lick the blood of her dead son with her tongue because it was her own blood. The reason she gives to her neighbor in the final scene of the play for not wanting to see her cry over the death of the Bridegroom is that "*vuestras lágrimas son lágrimas de los ojos nada más, y las mías vendrán cuando yo esté sola, de las plantas de los pies, de mis raíces, y serán más ardientes que la sangre*" (1267; your tears are only tears of the eyes and nothing more, and mine will come when I am alone, from the soles of my feet, from my roots, and they will be hotter than blood). The Bridegroom is well aware that he does not exist alone but as part of his ancestry. He says to the First Young Man, whom he meets in the woods while he is trying to find his Bride, "*¿Ves este brazo? Pues no es mi brazo. Es el brazo de mi hermano y el de mi padre y el de toda mi familia que está muerta*" (1252; Do you see this arm? Well, it is not my arm. It is my brother's arm and my father's and that of my whole family that is dead). The Mother also believes early in the play that she can have an idea of her daughter-in-law-to-be if she can learn something about the young woman's mother. She learns that the mother was beautiful but prideful. The Mother then suspects that the Bride will follow suit.

In *Yerma*, the talk of good and bad blood or strong and weak seed is an effort to place the blame for Yerma's barren state. The play traces the woman's untiring efforts to understand her barren state; even after she learns that husband and wife must be united in joyful, sexual union to produce a child, she relentlessly continues her effort to find out whose fault it is that she is not a mother. Chapter 5 indicated that Yerma does not feel like a real woman; Chapter 4 showed the lengths she goes to in her attempt to conceive a child. This chapter discusses the attempts by her and her neighbors to attribute guilt for her barrenness.

The Washerwomen cannot agree on whether or not Yerma is at fault. While one exonerates Yerma of all blame, another states that women who want to have children, do. The one who holds Yerma blameless places the fault on Juan for not giving Yerma children. The other insists that Yerma is guilty because of the flint she has for a tongue; she does not possess the tenderness of a mother. The Old Woman puts the blame squarely on Juan when she tells Yerma,

> *La culpa es de tu marido. . . . Ni su padre, ni su abuelo, ni su bis-abuelo se portaron como hombres de casta. Para tener un hijo ha sido necessario que se junte el cielo con la tierra. Están hechos de saliva. En cambio, tu gente no. Tienes hermanos y primos a cien leguas a la redonda. Mira que maldición ha venido a caer sobre tu hermosura* (1344; The fault is your husband's. . . . Neither his fa-ther, nor his grandfather, nor his great-grandfather behaved like

men of good caste. To have a child it has been necessary to unite the heaven with the earth. They are made of saliva. On the other hand, not so with your people. You have brothers and cousins for a hundred miles around. Look at what a curse has come to fall upon your beauty).

Juan, in his attempt to make his wife understand once and for all that she must accept the fact that they are never going to have children and that he prefers life that way, tells her point blank, "*No tenemos culpa ninguna*" (1348; We do not have any fault). Be that as it may, they have reached the end of their line: there will be no new generation in their family. That is not so much Yerma's concern, as it is the Mother's and María Josefa's.

Such is also the case in Bernarda Alba's house. While three generations of women live together, there will not be a fourth, María Josefa's protests notwithstanding. However strong their seed may have been in the past (Bernarda has given birth to five daughters and María Josefa inherited her strength from her father), there will be no descendants.

An additional thread among the plays is the theme of destiny. It is, in fact, the characters' attempts to control their own lives that come into conflict with the inevitable and bring about the final tragedies.[2] From the opening moments of *Blood Wedding*, and certainly with the first mention of knives, it is apparent that the characters will be victims of forces that they cannot control. Both Leonardo's wife and one of the Woodcutters state that these characters' lives are controlled by destiny. The Wife knows that her mother's fate will also be her own; one woodcutter knows that the fate that awaits the Bridegroom—his immediate death—is a part of his heritage, and that nothing can stop the force of the inevitable. What the Neighbor did not like about the Bride's mother was that she never loved her husband. Such is also the case with the Bride, who has also inherited her mother's haughtiness. Yerma's problem, in the largest sense, is that she is trying to go against fate, and that is impossible. From the play's title to Yerma's first mention of how many days she has been married, the reader knows that the inevitable for her is a sterile existence. As one of the Washerwomen observes, "*Todo esto son cuestiones de gente que no tiene conformidad con su sino*" (1304; All of this is a matter of people who do not conform to their destinies). In *Bernarda Alba,* destiny is intermingled with the repetition of the life cycle. The story of Adelaida and her past is the theme of destiny in microcosm. All the women in her family suffered before her, and she is destined to suffer, too. The single woman who killed her baby is another victim of her ancestry and her destiny. Her mother's name, *La Librada,* (the Liberated Woman?) suggests that she too had given birth to her daughter without the benefit of matrimony.

It was appropriate to begin this chapter with the theme of frustration, with which each of the plays begins. It is now appropriate to end this chapter with a discussion of the theme of death, with which each play ends. The foreshadowing of the Bridegroom's death begins when the Mother continually reminds us that he is the last man left in her family, the only chance for the continuation of the family line. That the Bride's secret love turns out to be a member of the same clan that killed the other two men in the Mother's family makes the death of the Bridegroom seem inevitable. But Lorca insisted on a certain poetic justice and had Leonardo and the Bridegroom kill each other.[3] Not only is the Mother left without a man in her home, but so is the Bride.

The intensity of frustration and mounting inevitability are the causes of the death in *Yerma* and *The House of Bernarda Alba.* There is no escape for Yerma; she is a prisoner of her barrenness and the husband who helps keep her in that state. What drives Yerma to commit murder is that her husband is not only satisfied but happy about their childless lives. Yerma knows that as long as he is alive she will suffer the anguish of hope that one day she may become a mother.

Adela's situation parallels Yerma's. She too is a prisoner of a situation that offers no hope and no other exit. The deaths in these plays are the needless destruction of three men and one woman who are in the prime of their lives. These characters are also the helpless victims of their own destinies.

Themes

Lorca crafted fine structure, etched masterful characterizations, and provided thought-provoking themes. But where he shone brightest was in the creation of the imagery and techniques that enhance the other aspects of his plays. They will be the subject of the next chapter.

chapter 7

Style: Techniques and Images

The techniques and images that a writer employs are designed to enhance and underscore the plot, characters, and themes in the work. Lorca was especially skillful and successful in his use of imagery and stagecraft, in part because he was a poet before he was a playwright. It is not always easy with Lorca's theater—the work of a poet—to distinguish between his dramatic techniques and his poetic imagery; imagery is, after all, one of the techniques. It is also difficult at times to distinguish among his characters, techniques, and images. Are the Woodcutters and the Moon in *Blood Wedding* characters, techniques for visual effect, or symbols of death? Is Yerma important in and of herself or as a symbol of a barren woman? Is Pepe el Romano a character in *The House of Bernarda Alba?* He sets the action of the play in motion but never appears onstage. Is his absence from the stage one of the techniques of stagecraft? Or is he a symbol of manhood? It is the task of this chapter to list and analyze Lorca's techniques and images and both to separate and integrate them.

The first element that the reader encounters upon opening the text of the plays is the list of characters, which is a good place to begin a discussion of the images and techniques. There is nothing haphazard in Lorca's choice of names for his characters. In *Blood Wedding,* one is struck by the fact that only Leonardo has a proper name; all the other characters bear names that define their functions or relationships. The first one listed is the *Madre* (Mother). Her name gives the reader a clue to her role. She is not called the *Viuda* (Widow) or the *Vieja* (Old Woman) because those functions are secondary for her to that of being a mother, which is her present and most important function in the play. She may even be the archetypal mother whose job it is to nurture and whose destiny it is to suffer because of what happens to her son, who is both the center of her life and her hope for the future.

The second character listed, seemingly in order of importance (certainly not in order of appearance), is the *Novia,* whose name may be ambiguously translated as either Bride or Girlfriend. By the second act of the play she is a wife, but she is not referred to as either the *Esposa* or the *Mujer* (Wife) the two Spanish words that signify that role in life. Her designation as the Bride shows that she never moves beyond the role of bride to the role of wife; her designation as the Girlfriend makes her as related to Leonardo as to the Bridegroom.

It becomes clear on arriving at the third character that they are not listed in order of importance; surely the Bridegroom or Leonardo should hold that place. The characters are instead grouped by sex: all the female characters are listed before any of the male characters. The symbolic characters appear at the end of the list. The third character is the *Suegra* (Mother-in-Law), defined in terms of her relationship to Leonardo, whose name the reader has not yet seen. She takes precedence in listing, if not in importance, over the *Mujer de Leonardo* (Wife of Leonardo), who is also defined in terms of a character still unfamiliar to the reader of the play. Perhaps because of her station in life, she appears before the *Criada* (Maid), who works for the Bride.

In the listing of the men, Leonardo appears before the Bridegroom. Why should Lorca have singled him out for a proper name, which derives from the Spanish word *león* (lion)? Perhaps it was the author's way of showing that Leonardo, more than any other character, is central to setting the play in motion—that is, to establishing a motivation for the Bride's act, which leads to the death of the two men in her life. The animal imagery of his name makes him stronger and more forceful than the "human" characters in the play. He is the king of beasts.

After the listing of the "real" characters, Lorca listed the metaphoric or symbolic characters, all of which represent death. Among them are the *Leñadores* (Woodcutters), who appear in a scene that takes place in a forest represented on stage by tree trunks. Early in the play, the Mother speaks of her dead son and husband as being represented by two trees near her house. The Woodcutters are searching for the Bridegroom, the Bride, and Leonardo so that they can cut them out of life. The objects in this forest are not living, full-sized trees but only stumps. The Woodcutters show what is to become of the characters they seek. They talk of blood and of death. Their accomplice is the *Luna* (Moon). The moon has a rich tradition in Lorca's poetry and serves the function here that it does there: it provides light at night for evil deeds—in this case, a duel to the death.[1] It speaks in poetry of death by knife. There is a crescendo in the scene in which these characters appear. First the Woodcutters occupy the stage, followed later by the Moon. The last symbolic character to make an appearance is the *Mendiga* (Beggar Woman), who is the physical representation of death and is so listed (*Muerte*) in the program. All these characters work in concert: the Woodcutters find the victim, the Moon lights the way, the Beggar Woman takes their lives.

This first scene of act 3 uses special effects to produce total theater: lights, sounds, poetry, and imagery. It is experimental theater and representative of the surrealist period of the 1930s in which it was written. The scene is highly stylized and poetic and has come to symbolize all that Lorca could do with the stage. For Lorca, it symbolized what he later wanted to get away from in his theater: *Yerma* would have no overtly surrealistic characters, and *The House of Bernarda Alba* would have no speeches in verse.[2] The prose of the third play is so highly polished that it gives the impression of being spontaneous conversation.

There is also symbolism in the names in *Yerma,* beginning with the title character, whose name reflects her role and her problem in life. As in *Blood Wedding*, Lorca listed all the women in the cast before he listed the men. The second name listed is that of María. María is the mother of a newborn baby, and her name is certainly intended to call to mind her namesake in the Gospels. The opening stage direction, in which Yerma sees a shepherd with a child dressed all in white, is a foreshadowing of the abundant Christological imagery in the play. In strong contrast to the religious image of María is the Old Woman, listed in the cast as *Vieja Pagana* (Old Pagan Woman); she states in the course of the play that she has never liked God. She transports the play out of a small Spanish village and into a more generalized locale. The name of the conjurer is Dolores, which means *pains* in Spanish and derives from the Mater Dolorosa (who seems to bear no resemblance to this character). Juan is the most common of masculine names in Spanish. Perhaps he is intended to be an Everyman, as Cahn called Yerma an Everywoman.[3] Víctor may be a form of the Spanish word for *victory*, but there seems to be little resemblance between his name and his function. *Yerma*, unlike *Blood Wedding*, has archetypal more than symbolic characters in the third act: the figures of the *Macho* (Male) and the *Hembra* (Female) embody the biological roles of the two sexes. Like the symbolic characters in *Blood Wedding*, the Male and the Female speak in poetry, or rather, sing in song. Each carries a large mask, which the playwright described as being both beautiful and full of the sense of earth and of nature. While the Female wears bells as a necklace, the Male carries a bull's horn whose phallic imagery is implicit. The children watching see the Male and the Female as the devil and his wife. (The songs that they sing are discussed later in this chapter.)

The most interesting of the minor characters are the six *Lavanderas* (Washerwomen). They are meant to serve the function of the chorus in Greek tragedy and may be intended to be symbolic characters. They comment on the action and represent the voice of the town's opinion of the heroine. They are also the play's finest touch and most poetic element, at once combining the common folks with high poetry.

It is in *The House of Bernarda Alba* that Lorca made the greatest

103

use of onomastic imagery and attributed character traits through the names. The eldest daughter is called Angustias; her name means *anguish*, and it characterizes her personality. The name of the second eldest, Magdalena, derives from Mary Magdalene. The name may seem to be a curious choice for this character, since she has no sexual past. She does have a low tolerance for hypocrisy and speaks out when Martirio and Amelia make hypocritical remarks. It is she who most misses her father, who cries for him at home, and who faints during the funeral. She is not afraid to face and speak the truth. For example, she knows that she is never going to marry; she tells Adela of Pepe's intention to marry Angustias; she sees Pepe for what he is; she does not believe that Angustias's wedding will take place; she sees the evil in Martirio's soul; and she curses the fate of being a woman. She has a good heart and would like to be able to do something to make Adela happy. The symbolism of Martirio's name is obvious: her name means martyrdom. She is the daughter who from the start claims not to be affected by the oppressive heat and not to need a fan to cool herself; she has little faith in life and acts mechanically; she will not admit that the medication that she is taking is doing her any good; and she claims not to care that she has no boyfriend. It is she who most suffers, even more than Angustias, from Adela's affair with Pepe. Martirio's name derives from the Greek word for *martyr*, meaning "to witness." It is Martirio's misfortune to have to bear witness to Adela's affair with Pepe, the man she also loves and desires.[4]

Adela's name is composed of the first five letters of the Spanish word *adelantar* ("to move forward"). In this case there is a perfect correlation between name and personality. She breaks with the past and forges ahead to the future by performing the symbolic act of breaking her mother's cane of authority and by ignoring the sexual mores of her society. She is not bound by tradition and writes her own rules for her life. She has to die at the end of the play because she is ahead of her time and cannot fit into her society.

Lorca's choice of name for the neighbor, Prudencia (Prudence), indicates his approval of her attitudes. She wants to forgive and forget and live in peace with her daughter, a stand that her honor-bound husband cannot adopt. There is much to be said about Bernarda's surname, Alba.[5] It is a poetic term used to designate *white*. As such, it fits in with the color symbolism of black and white in the play. It may be the white of purity or of hypocrisy. María Josefa combines the names of both parents of Jesus (Josefa is the feminine form of José, Joseph). She is the voice of truth in the drama and symbolically plays mother to a lamb that she pretends is her baby and says she is taking to Belén (Bethlehem).

A dramatic technique found to one degree or another in each of the three plays is the use of songs or poems. In *Blood Wedding*, they occur at both the tenderest and the tensest moments in the action. The first song is a lullaby sung by Leonardo's mother-in-law and wife to the baby. The lullabies of Lorca's native Andalusia were important to him. He once gave a lengthy lecture on those songs, and the lullaby in *Blood Wedding* is a form of one of the songs that he quoted in his speech.[6] (The song is replete with imagery that will be discussed later in this chapter.)

The second song is sung on the occasion of the Bride's wedding. The Maid begins the song, which is later repeated by the voices of the neighbors who have come for the wedding.

> *Despierte la novia*
> *la mañana de la boda.*
> *¡Que los ríos del mundo*
> *lleven tu corona!*
> . . . .
> *Que despierte*
> *con el ramo verde*
> *del laurel florido.*
> *¡Que despierte*
> *por el tronco y la rama*
> *de los laureles!*
> (1209–10)

> (Let the bride wake up
> on the morning of the wedding.

105

Let the rivers of the world
bring your crown!
. . . .
(Let her wake up
with the green branch
of the floral laurel.
Let her wake up
for the trunk and the branch
of the laurels!)

The first song is sung with tenderness, the second with joy. The Maid sings the third song while she is setting the table. It is a lengthy number that begins,

Giraba,
giraba la rueda
y el agua pasaba,
porque llega la boda,
que se aparten las ramas
y la luna se adorne
por su blanca baranda.
(1225–26)

(It was turning,
the wheel was turning
and the water was passing,
because the wedding is arriving,
let the branches separate
and the moon adorn itself
with its white railing.)

There are examples of unconscious irony in the song. What is turning is the Bride, from one man to another, and the moon that is adorning itself will be the accomplice in the death of both men. The song continues:

Cantaban,
cantaban los novios

y el agua pasaba,
porque llega la boda,
que relumbre la escarcha
y se llenen de miel
las almendras amargas.
(1226)

(They were singing,
the lovers were singing
and the water was passing,
because the wedding is arriving,
let the frost shine brightly
and the bitter almonds
be filled with honey.)

Again there is irony in the song relative to the events that are to follow. These lovers do not sing, and the Bride cannot tolerate her maid's questions about the wedding or even feign happiness. There will be nothing filled with honey—much less a honeymoon—or any sweetness at all.

The song ends talking of how her husband will be her protector and how she will live forever in his house.

Porque llega tu boda
recógete las faldas
y bajo el ala del novio
nunca salgas de tu casa.
Porque el novio es un palomo
con todo el pecho de brasa
y espera el campo el rumor
de la sangre derramada.
(1226)

(Because your wedding is arriving
gather up your skirts
and under the wing of your groom
you will never leave your house.
Because the groom is a dove

with a chest of red-hot coal
and the field waits for the sound
of the spilled blood.)

The Bride will never enter the Bridegroom's house while he is alive or
ever come under his protection; she does not think of him in the masculine terms of having a red-hot body. The only image that will be true
from this stanza is that of the spilled blood, a further example of unconscious irony.

The poetry in the third act serves the purposes of adding yet another element of stylization to the metaphorical characters, of height-
ening the tension of the first scene, and of expressing the love and
devotion between the Bride and Leonardo. The three woodcutters do
not begin speaking in verse until they see the arrival of the light of the
Moon, which, they say, *"llena de jazmines la sangre"* (1248; fills the
blood with jasmine).

The Moon's song describes her as a

> *Cisne redondo en el río,*
> *ojo de las catedrales,*
> *alba fingida en las hojas*
> *soy; ¡no podrán escaparse!*
> (1249)

> (Round swan in the river,
> the eye of the cathedrals,
> feigned white in the leaves
> I am; they will not be able to escape!)

She then refers back to the image of the knife that set in motion the
Mother's thoughts on death in the first scene of the play:

> *La luna deja un cuchillo*
> *abandonado en el aire,*
> *que siendo acecho de plomo*
> *quiere ser dolor de sangre.*
> (1249)

(The moon leaves a knife
abandoned in the air,
which being a spy of lead
wants to be the pain of blood.)

The knife is referred to here as a symbol of destruction hovering about and waiting to be the object of pain, blood, and death. The Moon then describes herself as death in its most mysterious form:

¡Dejadme entrar! Vengo helada
por paredes y cristales!
¡Abrid tejados y pechos
donde pueda calentarme!
¡Tengo frío! Mis cenizas
de soñolientos metales
buscan la cresta del fuego
por los montes y las calles.
(1249)

(Let me enter! I come frozen
through walls and windows!
Open roofs and chests
where I can warm myself!
I am cold! My ashes
of sleepy metals
search for the crest of the fire
through the mountains and the streets.)

These images of death are traditional in literature: the cold and ashes are in constant search for a place to rest. The image of the ashes and fire of death figure in another Spanish play, perhaps the most famous, *Don Juan Tenorio*. In José Zorrilla's nineteenth-century romantic drama—presented all over the Spanish-speaking world on All Soul's Day—Don Juan's imminent death is represented by his symbolic meal of fire and ashes.

The Moon knows that before the night is over her thirst for blood and need for warmth will be satisfied.

> *Pues esta noche tendrán*
> *mis mejillas roja sangre,*
> . . . .
> *¡No haya sombra ni emboscada,*
> *que no puedan escaparse!*
> *Que quiero entrar en un pecho*
> *para poder calentarme!*
> *Un corazón para mí!*
> *¡Caliente! . . .*
> (1250)

> (Well tonight
> my cheeks will have red blood,
> . . . .
> Let there be neither shadow nor ambush
> that will be able to escape me.
> I want to enter a chest
> in order to warm myself!
> A heart for me!
> Warm! . . .)

The heart is a symbol of life and death. It keeps the body alive by pumping blood, and the body dies when it stops. Someone else's death represents Death's (the Moon's) life. In her final lines, she speaks of one more symbol that needs to be mentioned here, since it is an important part of the play's imagery. "*Yo haré lucir al caballo / una fiebre de diamantes*" (1250; I shall light up the horse / a fever of diamonds). (The figure of the horse will be discussed later in this chapter.)

The most extensive and important use of poems and songs occurs in *Yerma*, in which the seven songs in the text serve to further the plot, define the characters, underscore the theme, and present the imagery. The whole story of the play (or "tragic poem") may well be contained in the opening stage direction, the lullaby, and the first few lines of dialogue. A shepherd enters the stage on tiptoes leading a child dressed all in white. Yerma awakens from her dream and sings the following song, which the reader must see in the original Spanish to appreciate both the rhythm and the meaning. The word *nana* means *lullaby*.

Style: Techniques and Images

A la nana, nana, nana,
a la nanita le haremos
una chocita en el campo
y en ella nos meteremos.
(1273)

(We'll make a cabin in the country for the new little mother and keep ourselves in it.) The poem expresses Yerma's fantasy of being a mother; her fantasy is unfortunately in direct opposition to the reality of her life.

After Juan leaves to work in the country, the second major stage direction is followed by the second song. Yerma runs her hand over her belly and engages in an imaginary dialogue with her nonexistent child:

¿De dónde vienes, amor, mi niño?
De la cresta del duro frío.
¿Qué necesitas, amor, mi niño?
La tibia tela de tu vestido.
(1277)

(Where do you come from, my love, my child?
From the crest of the cold marsh.
What do you need, my love, my child?
The tepid fabric of your dress.)

In Yerma's imagination, then, she needs a child who also needs her, especially the warmth—both physical and emotional—of a loving mother. She continues with the song's refrain: "¡*Que se agiten las ramas al sol / y salten las fuentes alrededor!*" (1277; Let the branches rustle in the sky / and let the waters jump about!)

If she can have a child, she will join the rest of the world around her—the trees and the water—and even nature will rejoice in her happiness. She also foresees what life might be like with a child in the house:

> *En el patio ladra el perro,*
> *en los árboles canta el viento.*
> *Los bueyes mugen al boyero*
> *y la luna me riza los cabellos.*
> *¿Qué pides, niño, desde tan lejos?*
> (1277)

> (On the patio the dog is howling,
> in the trees the wind sings.
> The oxen moo at their keeper
> and the moon makes my hair stand on end.
> What do you ask for, my child, from so far away?)

Yerma is a willing "mother," prepared to provide her child with anything he needs; all she needs to know are the child's needs. The supposed needs of the child also serve her own physiological and emotional needs: "*Los blancos montes que hay en tu pecho*" (1277; The white mountains that are on your chest). Thus, Yerma's body becomes the source of sustenance for her child and for her needs to nurture and feed. She then reveals her deepest feelings, which only the child can understand.

> *Te diré, niño mío, que sí,*
> *tronchada y rota soy para ti.*
> *¡Cómo me duele esta cintura*
> *donde tendrás primera cuna!*
> *¿Cuándo, mi niño, vas a venir?*
> (1278)

> (I'll tell you, my child, Yes,
> I am shattered and broken for you.
> How this waist aches for you
> where you will have your first cradle!
> When, my child, are you going to arrive?)

Since Yerma is inventing all the dialogue, the child answers as poetically as she does. "*Cuando tu carne huela a jazmín*" (1278; When your skin smells of jasmine). There is a paradox here: the child will arrive when Yerma has taken on—become—the fragrance of nature, but she cannot become a part of nature without first having a child. Of course, just being pregnant is enough to make her feel that she is a part of the world around her.

Yerma sings the first two songs alone—they are both a part of her fantasy life. The third song is a duet between Yerma and Víctor; if they had married, the song goes, he would not be alone in life. The idea is also expressed that Víctor belongs with Yerma, and she with him. Víctor begins the song:

> *¿Por qué duermes solo, pastor?*
> *¿Por qué duermes solo, pastor?*
> *En mi colcha de lana*
> *dormirás mejor.*
> *¿Por qué duermes, solo, pastor?*
> (1295)

> (Why are you sleeping alone, shepherd?
> Why are you sleeping alone, shepherd?
> In my woolen quilt
> you would sleep better.
> Why are you sleeping alone, shepherd?)

How convenient it is that the song is about a shepherd. Not only is Víctor a shepherd in the play, but the figure who appears to Yerma in her dream in the opening sequence is a shepherd, too. The following stanzas use imagery out of nature to depict how harsh Víctor's life is and how much more pleasant it could be if he lived with Yerma. She sings in reply to Víctor's opening stanza:

> *Tu colcha de oscura piedra,*
> *pastor,*
> *y tu camisa de escarcha,*
> *pastor,*
> *juncos grises del invierno*
> *en la noche de tu cama.*

> *Los nobles ponen agujas,*
> *pastor,*
> *debajo de tu almohada,*
> *pastor,*
> *y si oyes voz de mujer*
> *es la rota voz del agua.*
> *Pastor, pastor.*
>
> *¿Qué quiere el monte de ti?,*
> *pastor.*
> *Monte de hierbas amargas,*
> *¿qué niño te está matando?*
> *¡La espina de la retama!*
> (1295–96)

> (Your blanket of dark rock,
> shepherd,
> and your shirt of frost,
> shepherd,
> grey bulrushes of winter
> in your bed at night.
> The oak trees put needles
> shepherd,
> under your pillow,
> shepherd,
> and if you hear a woman's voice
> it is the broken voice of water.
> Shepherd, shepherd.
>
> What does the mountain want of you?,
> shepherd?
> Mountain of bitter grasses,
> what child is killing you?
> The thorn of the Spanish broom!)

The imagery makes the message clear that Víctor should not be sleeping where he is at the mercy of the pains of nature—a blanket of rocks, needles under his pillow, bitter herbs, and thorns. He should be sleeping in Yerma's "woolen quilt" between her "mountains." The sexual images are obvious and symbolize what could bring comfort to both Víctor and Yerma—and perhaps a child.

The second act begins with the song of the Washerwomen; this voice of society, this group that functions as a Greek chorus, sings with imagery, again, out of the world of nature.

> *En el arroyo frío*
> *lavo tu cinta,*
> *como un jazmín caliente*
> *tienes la risa.*
> (1300)

> (In the cold arroyo
> I wash your ribbon,
> and you have the laugh
> of hot jasmine.)

This is not the first time that Lorca used the image of jasmines. It also appears in the imaginary dialogue between Yerma and her unconceived child. The Washerwomen also sing of Juan and how he must work to protect his honor. Once again, they use an image out of the plant world: "*Yo planté un tomillo, yo lo vi crecer. / El que quiera honra, que se porte bien*" (1301; I planted some thyme, I watched it grow. / Let the man who wants honor conduct himself well). One reaps in life exactly what one sows. Honor does not just come to a man: he must plant its seeds and nurture them to see them develop into what he wants in life. In singing about Yerma, the Washerwomen use the opposite kind of imagery: "*¡Ay de la casada seca! / ¡Ay de la que tiene los pechos de arena!*" (1307; Woe to the dried-up wife! /Woe to the woman who has breasts of sand!). Just as *Yerma* means *barren*, so her breasts, which do not nourish children, resemble the sands of a desert. The Washerwomen's description of how conception takes place likens the sexual organs to flowers and birds.

> *Hay que pintar flor con flor*
> *cuando el verano seca la sangre al segador.*

Y abrir el vientre a pájaros sin sueño
cuando a la puerta llama temblando el invierno.
(1308)

(You have to join flower to flower
when the summer dries up the blood for the harvest.

And open your womb to sleepless birds
when winter trembles at the door.)

After a confrontation with Juan in the second scene of act 2, Yerma expresses in verse—and poetry—what is missing in her life:

¡Ay, qué prado de pena!
¡Ay, que puerta cerrada a la hermosura!
que pido un hijo que sufrir, y el aire
me ofrece dalias de dormida luna.
Èstos dos manantiales que yo tengo
de leche tibia son en la espesura
de mi carne dos pulsos de caballo
que hacen latir la rama de mi angustia.
¡Ay, pechos ciegos baja mi vestido!
¡Ay, palomas sin ojos ni blancura!
¡Ay, qué dolor de sangre prisionera
me está clavando avispas en la nuca!
(1316)

(Oh, what a meadow of pain!
Oh, what a door closed to beauty!
I ask only to suffer a child, and the air
offers me dahlias of a sleeping moon.
These two sources that I have
of tepid milk are in the thicket
of my flesh two horses' pulses
that make the boughs of my anguish throb.
Oh, blind breasts under my dress!
Oh, doves without eyes or whiteness!
Oh, what pain of blood kept prisoner
are asps clawing my nape!)

Style: Techniques and Images

Again, the images are but of nature. Her breasts, which could be doves of joy for a child, are blind to their function. Doves that could be symbols of peace keep her at war with herself. She is the victim of the pulse of horses in her breasts and the prisoner of asps that torment her in her blood and on her body. It is in the final lines of the poem that Yerma expresses her feeling of having being divorced from nature:

> Pero tú has de venir, amor, mi niño,
> porque el agua da sol, la tierra fruta,
> y nuestro vientre guarda tiernos hijos,
> como la nube lleva dulce lluvia.
> (1316)

> (But you have to come, my love, my child,
> because the water gives salt, the land fruit,
> and our wombs hold tender children,
> and the cloud carries sweet rain.)

Only *she* is without a function in this world; she has been made to serve a purpose but cannot perform it. She is without the job of carrying the sweetness of rain, the fruit of the trees, or even the salt of the water. She feels useless.

The last songs appear in the final scene at the fertility rite. Lorca opened the scene with the chant that describes the purpose of the ritual:

> No te pude ver
> cuanndo eras soltera,
> mas de casada
> te encontraré.
> Te desnudaré,
> casada y romera,
> cuado en lo oscuro
> las doce den.
> (1336)

> (I could not see you
> when you were single;

but I shall find you,
the married woman.
I shall undress you,
married pilgrim,
when in the dark of night
the clock strikes twelve.)

It is clear from the song that only married women who have not been able to become pregnant through any other means (including potions and prayers) finally make the pilgrimage to avail themselves of the men eager to try to impregnate them. The spectacle begins with the parade of barefooted women carrying candles and praying in song. To Yerma belong the first two and last two lines of the following chant:

Señor, que florezca la rosa,
no me dejéis en sombra.

Sobre su carne marchita
florezca la rosa amarilla.

Y en el vientre de tus siervos
la llama oscura de la tierra.
(1338)

(Lord, who makes the rose flower,
do not leave mine in the shadow.

Upon her withered flesh
make the yellow rose bloom.

And in the womb of your servants
ignite the dark flame of the earth.)

As previously, the images in the women's prayers come from the world of nature, specifically from the flora. In the request to have the flame of the earth in their wombs, the earth, on which Yerma has walked barefooted to absorb its powers, is seen as a symbol of fertility. Finally, Yerma recites her own personal prayer:

Style: Techniques and Images

El cielo tiene jardines
con rosales de alegría,
entre rosal y rosal
la rosa de maravilla.
Rayo de aurora parece
y un arcángel la vigila,
las alas como tormentas,
los ojos como agonía.
Alrededor de sus hojas
arroyos de leche tibia
juegan y mojan la cara
de las estrellas tranquilas.
Señor, abre tu rosal
sobre mi carne marchita.
(1338–39)

(The sky has gardens
with rosebushes of happiness,
between one bush and another
the rose of marvel.
A ray of dawn appears,
and an archangel keeps guard over it,
the wings as turmoil,
the eyes as agony.
Around its leaves
arroyos of warm milk
play and wet the faces
of the tranquil stars.
Lord, open your rosebush
upon my withered skin.)

The equation is clear: pregnancy is the flowers of the garden; the garden of rosebushes is true happiness. The one rose that parts the other is the object of marvel. It contains the ray of hope, a hope so precious that a special angel stands guard over it. The rosebush makes flowers out of withered flesh.

Finally, there are the songs of the Female and the Male, earthy and sensual songs about the roles of the sexes and about mating. The Female sings first:

En el río de la sierra
la esposa triste se bañaba.
Por el cuerpo le subían
los caracoles del agua.
La arena de las orillas
y el aire de la mañana
le daban fuego a su risa
y temblor a sus espaldas.
¡Ay, qué desnuda estaba
la doncella en el agua!
(1340)

(In the mountain's river
the sad wife was bathing.
Along her body climbed
the snails from the water.
The sand of the shores
and the morning's air
gave fire to her laugh
and trembling to her shoulders.
Oh, how naked was
the maiden in the water!)

A section later in this chapter will explore the sexual associations of water. The meaning here is obvious: water has procreative powers, which is what attracts barren women to it. The snails, like the birds and the flowers, are an element of nature being contrasted with the barren sands of the shore (Yerma's breasts were previously compared to sand). Then it is the Male's turn to sing:

¡Ay, qué blanca
la triste casada!
¡Ay, cómo se queja entre las ramas!
Amapola y clavel será luego
cuando el macho despliegue su capa.
(1341)

(Oh, how white
the sad wife!

120

The final scene of *Yerma* as presented in Madrid in 1934. *Courtesy of the Fundación Federico García Lorca.*

> Oh, how she complains among the branches!
> Later she will be a poppy and a carnation
> when the male unfurls his cape.)

Juan is described as being white, Víctor as having a spot on his face from the sun. That spot represents the difference between sterility and virility. Here, as long as the wife remains white (unfertilized), she is unhappy and complains of how she is not a part of the branches (i.e., nature). She will only become a part of nature (a poppy, a carnation) when the male opens his clothing. He gets close to the Female and continues his erotic song:

> *Si tú vienes a la romería*
> *a pedir que tu vientre se abra,*
> *no te pongas un velo de luto,*
> *sino dulce camisa de holanda.*
> *Vete sola detrás de los muros,*

donde están las higueras cerradas,
y soporta mi cuerpo de tierra
hasta el blanco gemido del alba.
¡Ay, cómo relumbra!
¡Ay, cómo relumbraba,
ay, cómo se cimbrea la casada!
(1341)

(If you come to the pilgrimage
to ask that your womb be opened,
do not wear a veil of mourning,
but a shirt of fine chambray.
Go alone behind the walls,
where the closed fig trees are,
and support my body of earth
until the white sob of dawn.
Oh, how it shines!
Oh, how it shone!
Oh, how the married woman was thrashing about.)

Yerma had heard earlier that if she wants to become pregnant she must "sing" when she is in bed with her husband (that is, be joyful). The Male repeats the message in his admonition against wearing clothing that reflects sadness rather than sensuality and joy. When the women go off with the men who are waiting for them, they must be ready to accept the powers of the earth—the men's virility—all night long. There is an indication in the final line that what made one woman thrash about is also what was shining in the two previous lines, the male sex organ. Before the Male has a chance to finish his song, the Female interjects:

¡Ay, que el amor le pone
coronas y guirnaldas,
y dardos de oro vivo
en su pecho se clavan.
(1342)

(Oh, love puts
wreaths and garlands,

and darts of living gold
in the breast that they pierce.)

If the woman allows the act of love to take place and withstands the penetration of her body, she is rewarded with the laurels that the Greeks awarded to their prize-winning athletes. She becomes a true heroine worthy of merit and reward. But the woman cannot always take the entire act of lovemaking all at once:

> *Siete veces gemía,*
> *nueve se levantaba,*
> *quince veces juntaron*
> *jazmines con naranjas.*
> (1342)

> (Seven times she moaned,
> nine times she got up,
> fifteen times there was union
> between the jasmines and the oranges.)

Even the Female, the archetype of womanhood, must admit that "*como flor se cansa*" (1343; the flower is becoming tired) as the ritual comes to an end. The Male knows what effect he wants to have on the Female before their union ends.

> *Que se queme la danza*
> *y el cuerpo reluciente*
> *de la linda casada,*
> . . . .
> *El cielo tiene jardines*
> *con rosales de alegría,*
> *entre rosal y rosal*
> *la rosa de maravilla.*
> (1313)

> (Let the dance burn
> and the body of the pretty
> married woman become radiant.
> . . . .

> The sky has gardens
> with rosebushes of joy,
> between bush and bush,
> the rose of marvel.)

The Male sums up the man's role:

> *En esta romería*
> *el varón siempre manda.*
> *Los maridos son toros.*
> *El varón siempre manda,*
> *y las romeras flores,*
> *para aquel que las gana.*
> (1342)

> (At this ritual
> the male always rules.
> Husbands are bulls.
> The male always rules,
> the women who come are flowers,
> for the man who earns them.)

The images of women as flowers and flowers as symbols of virginity will also figure in the symbolism of one of the songs in *The House of Bernarda Alba.*

When Lorca was working on *Bernarda Alba,* he was intent upon keeping it free of poetry: he meant to eliminate the special effects and metaphorical characters that he used in the other two plays of the trilogy. The play contains, however, not only the touch of the poet in its very conception and execution but also four passages of verse, poetry, and song.[7] They are brief, but they underscore character traits and themes and contain important imagery. The first such passage is less a poem or song than a choral prayer. It occurs in the first act while the neighbors are at Bernarda's house after the funeral. They recite prayers in both Spanish and Latin for the soul of Bernarda's late husband. The passage is included in part to underscore Bernarda's hypocrisy. In front of the neighbors, she prays; in private, she is uncharitable. The second piece is the short song of the Reapers; the song is heard, but the singers are never seen on stage.

> *Ya salen los segadores*
> *en busca de las espigas;*
> *se llevan los corazones*
> *de las muchachas que miran.*
> (1486)

> (The reapers are now going
> in search of the spikes;
> they carry off the hearts
> of the girls who see them.)

Men in general, and the Reapers in particular, represent to Bernarda's daughters the freedom they do not have. The first stanza makes Adela realize how much of a prisoner she feels in the house where she does not have the freedom to come and go. The second stanza provokes in both Adela and Martirio the feelings of passion and nostalgia:

> *Abrir puertas y ventanas*
> *las que vivís en el pueblo,*
> *el segador pide rosas*
> *para adornar su sombrero.*
> (1487)

> (Open the doors and windows
> you women who live in town,
> the reaper asks for roses
> to adorn his hat.)

The image of the rose is used here like it is in *Yerma:* as a sexual symbol of womanhood, or virginity, after which the Reapers are chasing.

The third piece is a poem that reflects a Spanish tradition. On seeing a falling star, it is customary to recite: "*Santa Bárbara bendita / que en el cielo estás escrita / con papel y agua bendita*" (1516; Blessed

Saint Barbara / which is written in the sky / with paper and holy water). This poem allowed Lorca to contrast the personalities of Amelia and Adela. Amelia closes her eyes so that she will not see the light in the sky. Not Adela: "*A mí me gusta ver correr lleno de lumbre lo que está quieto y quieto anōs enteros*" (1516; I like to see running filled with light that which has been kept quiet for years and years). Adela questions traditions and transgresses them; she has little respect for local customs and none for Spanish mores.

The fourth song is María Josefa's and has already been mentioned in the discussion of onomastic imagery. She sings the following lullaby to the sheep that she has cradled in her arms:

> *Ovejita, niño mío,*
> *vámonos a la orilla del mar.*
> *La hormiguita estará en su puerta,*
> *yo te daré la teta y el pan.*
> (1523)

> (Little sheep, my child,
> let's go to the seashore.
> The little ant is in the doorway,
> and I shall give you breast and bread.)

The song shows María Josefa's maternal instincts, even at the age of 80. She has the facsimile of the child her granddaughters will never bear. Then she continues:

> *Bernarda,*
> *cara de leoparda.*
> *Magdalena,*
> *cara de hiena.*
> *¡Ovejita!*
> *Meee, meeee.*
> *Vamos a los ramos del portal de Belén.*
> (1523)

> (Bernarda,
> face of a leopard.

Style: Techniques and Images

Magdalena,
face of a hyena.
Little sheep!
Meee, meeee.
Let's go to the branches at the entrance to Bethlehem.)

Here she expresses her feelings against her daughter, on whom she puts the face of a leopard, and her granddaughter, who reminds her of a hyena. She also fulfills the expectations raised by her name; the sheep in her arms is meant to represent the baby Jesus. The song gives her a chance to tell Martirio the truth about the fate of the women languishing in Bernarda Alba's house.

The house is the central image in *Bernarda Alba.* Eric Bentley perceptively observed the important role of the windows and doors that serve as both barriers and bridges.[8] Students of the play should note that Lorca did not call his drama simply, *Bernarda Alba,* or even, *La familia de Bernarda Alba,* but rather, *La casa de Bernarda Alba.* Critics must therefore start with the title in any analysis of the imagery in the work.

The house is its own little society, a virtual dictatorship in which Bernarda rules. The physical house is the dividing line; it separates inside from outside. The walls keep Bernarda's secrets inside and the watchful eyes of the neighbors outside. Inside the house, the veneer of decency reigns; outside is the corruption. To Bernarda's way of thinking, virginity is decency and sex is corruption. It is understandable, therefore, that when Adela hangs herself, Bernarda's first thought should be to make the world believe that her daughter died a virgin. It is also logical that all the sexual activity takes place outside of the house. It is outside, in the corral, that Adela has her clandestine meetings with Pepe; outside that the single mother has to acknowledge her sin; there that Paca la Roseta spent a night with some men while her husband was tied to a tree; and, again, behind the corral that Bernarda's late husband used to raise the maid's petticoat.

The first stage direction of the play is a description of the physical house. "*Habitación blanquísima del interior de la casa Bernarda. Muros gruesos*" (1439; Intensely white room inside Bernarda's house.

127

Thick walls). In the note before the start of the play, "*el poeta* [*Lorca*] *advierte que estos tres actos tienen la intención de un documental fotográfico*" (1439; The poet [Lorca] advises that these three acts are meant to be a photographic document). In Lorca's days, photographs were in black and white. The stark whiteness of the house (also indicated by the word *alba*) serves as a striking contrast with the women dressed in the black clothing of mourning. What was Lorca's intention in making the room in the first act intensely white? There are several possibilities. First, it could suggest the purity and decency that Bernarda insists should prevail inside of her house. Secondly, it can suggest the whitewash of hypocrisy, which dominates the household. Thirdly, it can reflect the sun and intense heat of the Spanish summers. (An argument for the third point will follow later in this section.)[9]

The walls, described as thick, serve Bernarda's purpose of keeping her family's secrets contained within them. They also give rise to some of the metaphorical descriptions of the house, which is referred to alternately as a convent, a house of war, and hell itself; it is also a prison for Bernarda's mother and daughters.

The second act takes place in an "*habitación blanca*" (white room) near the bedrooms. The play is a penetration into the hearts, and an examination of the motives, of the inhabitants of the household. The house serves as a metaphor for that exploration. From the first act to the second, the family secrets have been partially exposed. It is therefore fitting that the setting should progress from a room near the entrance hall to the more intimate room that gives access to the bedrooms. In addition, the heat of the day is less intense in the second act than in the first, so the reflection of the sun is less pronounced on the walls.

By the third act, the reader is well acquainted with what the family is really all about, so the setting progresses to the part of the house that gives way to the corral. It is now nighttime, and the walls are tinged with blue. The color also suggests that the purity and decency that seemed to prevail early in the play are now tinged with more than just a shade of doubt. Only one other color appears in the play: the dress that Adela puts on after the funeral is green. Green is the color of nature, as well as of hope and even jealousy. In European literature, it has sexual connotations.

There is also a practical reason for the various settings of the three acts. The first act needs to take place in a room to which the mourners have immediate access upon returning from the funeral. The second act has to show La Poncia going from bedroom to bedroom in her search for the missing photograph of Pepe. The location of the third act has to give Adela a quick access to the corral for her rendezvous with Pepe. It is the house that keeps the daughters locked up away from the fresh air of freedom. (To a lesser extent, Yerma's house serves a similar function: she calls it a tomb and a place that is burning from within—something like hell.) Most important is that the house keep the women separated from men.[10]

The men in these plays are symbols more than fully developed characters. In the course of writing the three plays, Lorca was able to pare down the number of male characters from three (not counting the Woodcutters) in *Blood Wedding* to the two (not counting the Male) who contrast with each other in *Yerma,* and finally to no man setting foot onstage in *The House of Bernarda Alba.* The characters of the Bridegroom and Leonardo, Juan and Víctor, discussed as individuals in the preceding chapter, are important to this discussion because of their functions in the play and because they are two important male figures contrasting with each other. In the Bride's speech to the Mother at the end of *Blood Wedding,* she explains why she left her husband and ran off with Leonardo. She saw the Bridegroom as "*un poquito de agua*" (a little drop of water) who could not satisfy her needs as a woman. She wanted to have a "real man," and that was Leonardo. The Mother may have been unwittingly responsible for the way her son turned out as a man. She expresses her wish that he were a girl who would stay at home with her; she tries to keep him from going off to work in the field; she attempts to protect him from what she considers the impending disaster. At the meeting with the Bride's father, she does the talking for her son and presents him in a way that is inconsistent with the Spanish image of manhood. She talks of his never having had sexual contact with a woman and insists that he will not even drink a glass of wine at the Father's house. He is not his own man.

Not so with Leonardo. He may not be a character worthy of admiration, but he is independent, and there is no question about his physical or emotional strength. He is the kind of man who appeals to the Bride. (The Bride is such a strong character that even Leonardo takes a secondary place to her. It is she who initiates the flight, who prepares the horse, and who puts the spurs on Leonardo.) Part of Leonardo's masculinity is depicted in his insistence on traveling to the wedding by horse (a masculine symbol to be discussed soon) rather than in a carriage with his wife. The men in the play serve to set off the character of the Bride and to bring about the tragedy for the Mother; they are not important in and of themselves.

The situation is similar in *Yerma*. Juan, who is pale, is not the man who can make Yerma a mother. He is also too emotionally weak to control his wife's behavior and ultimately dies by her hands. In sharp contrast is the character of Víctor, who is sunburned and, on the one occasion when he held Yerma in his arms, made her tremble with joy.

There are no men in *The House of Bernarda Alba*, but they hover in the background and are a major source of conversation among the sisters. Pepe may well be the main character without even setting foot on the stage. It is he who sets the action of the play in motion. For all his importance in the play, the reader learns little about him. Such was Lorca's intention and method of maintaining his mystique. More than an individual, he is the symbol of manhood in the time and place that the play transpires. His absence from the stage is a major dramatic technique in the play. Lorca was writing a play in large measure about the sexual frustration of women in Spanish towns. What better way to keep the women frustrated than by eliminating men from the cast? And what better way could the playwright have found of maintaining the masculine mystique than by keeping Pepe from appearing onstage?

All that the reader knows about Pepe is that he is handsome, 25 years old, and the most desirable man for miles around—desirable, that is, at least physically. He also has no scruples. He is marrying

Angustias for her money and sleeping with her sister every night. It takes no more than the mention of his name to get the sisters in an uproar. When the Maid mentions that he is passing through the street, the sisters run to the window just to get a glimpse of him.

Pepe has pitted mother against daughter and sister against sister. His effect is especially notable on Adela and Martirio. Adela is prepared to betray anyone she has to in order to keep him. All he has to do is whistle (the only physical evidence that the audience has of his presence) to get Adela to meet him in the corral. Martirio can no longer see Adela as a sister, only as another woman, a rival for Pepe's attentions; with the possible exception of Adela, no one is fooled by the man's character. Magdalena knows that he is capable of anything, and even Martirio has to admit that he has no soul. It is María Josefa who gives the description of him, in the larger-than-life dimensions, that Lorca had in mind: "*Pepe el Romano es un gigante. Todas lo queréis. Pero el os va a devorar porque vosotras sois granos de trigo. No granos de trigo. Ranas sin lengua!*" (1525; Pepe el Romano is a giant. All of you want him. But he is going to devour you because you are grains of wheat. No, not grains of wheat. Frogs without tongues). No, the granddaughters are not grains of wheat, associated with the (re)productive natural world, but frogs that depend on their tongues for food, for life. Without their tongues, frogs die. María Josefa sees in her granddaughters the death of her family's line. As she views them, her granddaughters are defenseless against Pepe's powers. He shows that he is just another opportunist when Bernarda fires a shot and he takes off on his horse. Since he believes in nothing but his own preservation, there is nothing and no one for which he is willing to stand up and fight.

The picture of Pepe is no different from that of the other men of the town: they are all little better than animals, acting on instinct, ruled by the penis, not by the brain or the heart. The play is replete with examples: the men who carried off Paca la Roseta, and the men in Adelaida's past. Bernarda does not even allow the men to enter her house after the funeral; they must remain on the outside patio where she gives them a drink and then sends them away. She is constantly on guard against men and the effect that they can have on women. The only man a woman should look at in church is the priest because he wears a skirt. When the Reapers—compared with phallic imagery to "*árboles quemados*" (1485; trees on fire)—are in town, La Poncia warns the daughters not to open the door too wide because they might try to force themselves in and on the women. She knows that men are men and that women have to be careful not to provoke them. As she sees it, only men need sex, but it should not be denied to them. Now that the Reapers are in town, a prostitute has arrived. Years earlier, La Poncia gave her son money to pay for the woman's services because "*los hombres necesitan estas cosas*" (1486; Men need these things).

The men who are involved in scandalous activities do not come from Bernarda's town; they are always from far away. The Reapers have come down from the mountains, the men who went off with Paca are from another town, Adelaida's father was in Cuba when he murdered her mother's first husband. The men in Bernarda's town are not capable of doing more than watching "real" men engage women sexually and talk about what goes on around them. The reason has to do with water, which in Lorca's system of symbols is a sexual image, a source of potency. Since Bernarda's town is landlocked and does not have a river flowing through it, the men of her town are removed from the source of virility. When María Josefa talks of going off to get married, it is not with a local man but with a man who lives near the sea, so that she can have lots of children. The sea is a source of foam, and foam is likened to sperm. Color symbolism resurfaces in the sexual imagery: the black of repression versus the white of procreation. The two colors and images contrast with each other in Bernarda's closing speech of the play: "*Nos hundiremos todas en un mar de luto*" (1532; We shall all immerse ourselves in a sea of mourning). In *Yerma*, the heroine comments that Víctor's voice sounds like a current of water; that reference makes sense as a further testimony to his virility. And it becomes clear why the Bride refers to her husband—who, to her, lacks manly characteristics—as a little drop of water. A logical extension of the water imagery is Bernarda Alba's daughters drinking it in an attempt not just to quench their thirst but to lessen their sexual frustration (as discussed later).

María Josefa comments on the effect that a man has on a house full of single women. Adela speaks of how she drinks in Pepe's blood by looking into his eyes. Víctor, whose voice has the rumbling of water, is able to make Yerma "tremble." Leonardo attracts the Bride like the force of the sea.

If the house, men, and water are the principal symbols in *Bernarda Alba,* blood, knives, and horses are predominant in *Blood Wedding.* Blood appears in different contexts and in many of its associations. First there is the positive image of the bloodline that unites generation to generation, such as the Bridegroom to his father and his grandfather. Also positive is Leonardo's reference to himself as a "man of blood," that is, as honorable. But there is the negative association of blood with death, and that image appears in the lullaby that the Mother-in-Law sings, as well as in the wedding song that the Maid sings. In both, blood is a foreshadowing of the outcome of the play. In the lullaby, "*La sangre corría / más fuerte que el agua*" (1184; The blood was flowing / stronger than water), and in the wedding song, "*y espera el campo el rumor / de la sangre derramada*" (1226; and the field awaits the sound / of spilled blood), an event that is going to happen shortly after the wedding takes place.

The Bridegroom's mother and the Bride's father do not agree with Leonardo on his assessment of his blood. The Father knows that he has "bad blood" and will end up in disgrace. The Mother expects nothing else from him, since his blood is that of his family. Early in the play, there is a reference to the blood spilled by the Mother's husband and first son; she was willing to wet her hands with it and lick it off because their blood was also her blood. The other references to blood occur in the third act, in the context of death. A final association with blood is not stated but rather implied. When the Bride tells the Mother that she remains a chaste woman despite her marriage to the Bridegroom and her flight with Leonardo, she is referring to the blood of her virginity.

The symbolism of the knife is closely united with that of blood: it is the cause of death and the symbol with which the action of the play begins and ends. From the moment the Bridegroom asks for the knife to cut the vines and the Mother reacts emotionally, the knife becomes a symbol or tool of death. It is entirely fitting that the Bride-groom (and Leonardo) die in the manner that is suggested throughout the play—in a knife duel.[11]

The third important image is that of the horse. In *Bernarda Alba*, water is the principal symbol of masculinity; in *Blood Wedding*, it is the horse. Leonardo and his horse are closely identified with each other. The Mother-in-Law knows that Leonardo is up to trouble when she looks at the horse and sees that it is out of breath; she then knows how hard Leonardo has been riding it and can only guess at his destination. The horse is a symbol of force, speed, strength, and masculinity, and Lorca imparted these characteristics to Leonardo in part through the horse-rider identification. It is because the horse is a symbol of masculinity that Leonardo rides on it instead of in the less masculine carriage with his wife. The horse also serves to get Leonardo to the Bride's wedding early, and alone. There may be unconscious irony and foreshadowing in a casual comment that the Bride makes on Leonardo's arrival. She thinks that Leonardo is going to kill the horse with his wild riding. Leonardo's response is simply, "*¡Cuando se muera, muerto está!*" (1211; When he dies, he'll be dead!). Ironically enough, the horse outlives its master. Leonardo's wife notices that something is wrong and that her husband is gone from the wedding not just because she cannot find him but because she does not see his horse. When the Woodcutters are searching out Leonardo, what they listen for is the sound of his horse. Likewise, the Bridegroom does not hear Leonardo in the woods but does hear a horse, with which he associates the man. In the poetic scene between the Bride and Leonardo in act 3, Leonardo states that it was not he who went to her house, "*Pero montaba a caballo / y el caballo iba a tu puerta*" (1258; But I was mounted on the horse / and the horse was going to your door). The first reference to the horse appears in the Mother-in-Law's lullaby:

> *Duérteme, rosal,*
> *que el caballo se pone a llorar.*
> *Las patas heridas,*

> *las crines heladas,*
> *dentro de los ojos*
> *un puñal de plata.*
> *Bajaban al río.*
> *¡Ay, cómo bajaban!*
> *La sangre corría*
> *más fuerte que el agua.*
> (1184)

> (Sleep, rosebush,
> the horse is starting to cry.
> The hooves wounded,
> the mane frozen,
> in his eyes
> a silver dagger.
> They were going down to the river.
> Oh, how they were going!
> The blood was running
> stronger than water.)

And so all three images—horse, knife, and blood—are united in a seemingly innocent baby's lullaby.

Pepe el Romano is closely associated with his horse in much the same way that Leonardo is with his, thus forming a bond of identification between the two men. The discussion in act 2 of *Bernarda Alba* about the time when Pepe left Angustias's window is settled by the sound of his horse. Amelia heard the horse at 1:30 A.M., but La Poncia heard it at 4 A.M. The horse's strength and speed save Pepe's life by carrying him away when Bernarda tries to shoot him.[12]

There is no single image, such as a horse or a house, that predominates in *Yerma*. The character herself and her name are the major symbols. What serves to contrast with Yerma's barren state and to heighten her frustration is the whole of fruitful nature that surrounds her. Her speech, as already noted, is filled with references to the natural world, especially to flowers. Some add beauty to the world, such as the seemingly useless yellow *jaramango* hedge. The wind sings as it passes through the branches of trees. The jasmine adds a pleasant aroma to the world. Promoting procreation, the rose and its thorny bush become symbols for the sex organs.

In *Blood Wedding*, flowers have metaphorical value: men are likened to geraniums and handsome ones to flowers in general. Thus, there is a reversal of the traditional symbol of women being like flowers; the Mother's late husband, for instance, smelled of carnations. Babies are compared to carnations, roses, and dahlias. Flowers also serve as symbols in the sexual imagery, especially in the description of the stockings that the Bridegroom bought for his bride-to-be: a rose with its seeds and stem are woven right along the thigh. It is curious and ironic to note that floral imagery, a symbol of life, can also be associated with death. Adela dies after Martirio shows Bernarda the straw on her sister's clothes—the symbol of sin. Yerma dies spiritually when she realizes that she is worth less than a plant.

Animals and other natural elements of the universe serve both symbolic and practical functions. In *Blood Wedding*, the bull represents both a man and a wedding; the Bride is a dove. A man has the beauty of a nightingale's plumage, and a bride is crowned with orange blossoms.[13] There are other images out of nature: a man is a tree, a woman the earth and a star. The association with the land identifies woman as Earth Mother, whose beauty is comparable to that of a star. In *Bernarda Alba*, La Poncia compares herself to a loyal bitch, and a woman from the funeral compares Bernarda to a lizard. Bernarda sees no difference between the poor and a bunch of animals. It comes as no surprise that Pepe is compared to a lion, relating him, again, to *Blood Wedding*'s Leonardo. The specific reference shows men (which Pepe represents) as the basest of creatures. Adela tells Martirio in the third act that Pepe "*ahí fuera está, respirando como si fuera un león*" (1530; is outside there, breathing like a lion). Coming from any of the other women, the description could be considered a slam against men; from Adela, it merely describes him and his needs. Two animals in the play are representative of characters: during the scene in which Prudencia is having dinner at Bernarda's house, there is a loud bang against the walls. It is the stallion trying to break free. Curiously enough, Bernarda orders him released to the corral (the site of unleashed passion) before he breaks down the walls, which are her protection from the world outside. The horse is given human qualities when he is described as "*bregando como un hombre*" (1509; struggling like a man). The man he represents may very well be Pepe; if so, we have a reversal of roles: horse as man, rather than man as animal. He may also represent the daughters trying to break free of their mother's domination and the sexual oppression that is represented physically by the confines of the house. The other animal reference occurs when the sisters are talking about noises that they heard coming from the corral during the night. Amelia suggests that it might have been "*una mulilla sin desbravar*" (an untamed mule). Martirio knows that in fact it was Adela and says, "*Eso, ¡eso!, una mulilla sin desbravar*" (1489; That's it, that's it! an untamed mule). The untamed young mule is really the untamed young sister.

Animals, particularly dogs, have a practical function in *The House of Bernarda Alba*. It is the barking of the dogs in the corral that alerts La Poncia and the Maid to someone's presence there on the night that Pepe is supposed to be out of town. The barking is followed by the appearance of Adela, who allegedly cannot sleep because of thirst and wants a drink of water. The barking is the signal to her that Pepe is waiting. His whistle to her (the only sound he makes in the play) summons Adela as if she were a dog. There is also the dog in act 2 that digs up the body of the baby murdered by the single woman to hide her shame. And of course, there is the sheep that María Josefa mothers in the third act, and her references to Bernarda as a leopard and to Magdalena as a hyena.

Christian symbolism in the plays occurs not only in María Josefa's song; it also exists in references that the heroines make. The most notable example is in *Yerma:* the title character speaks of her breasts as blind doves after her neighbor María speaks of her son as a dove of light. Both *dove* and *light* refer to Jesus, who told his disciples to be as innocent as doves (Matt. 10:16); in addition, the Gospels of Mark (1:10), Luke (3:21–22), and John (1:32) relate that when Jesus was baptized, the Holy Spirit descended on him like a dove. The image of light is consistent with the illumination that radiated from the baby

Jesus. There is another Christian association with Yerma's dry and useless breasts: Jesus said to the daughters of Jerusalem, "Blessed be the barren woman, the wombs that never bore and the breasts that never nursed!" (Luke 23:24)[14] Yerma also speaks of suffering because of, and being martyrized by, a son. Ironically, it is Juan who is the martyr to his wife's suffering. His death, like that of Jesus, takes place on a mountaintop. Yerma speaks, too, of the cross she has to bear and of the nails in her body. Finally, she speaks of her crown of thorns and the hammer blows that she feels instead of the mouth of a sucking baby. Adela speaks of herself in similar terms, and the reader might ask if it would have been appropriate for *her* name to be Martirio— she dies for the cause of personal freedom. In the confrontation between Adela and Martirio, the former speaks of being "pursued by those who call themselves decent" and wearing the "crown of thorns that the mistresses of married men have" (cited earlier).

Lorca used a variety of devices to enhance the dramatic quality of his plays. In *Bernarda Alba,* the weather and the terminology about it figure prominently. To intensify the sexual discomfort of the women, Lorca set his play in the heat of the Spanish summer. There is a direct relationship between the physical heat and the sexual heat that the sisters suffer. The first confrontation between Adela and Bernarda is over the need for a fan to use against the summer's heat. Lorca prepared the reader for this unpleasant incident by having two women after the funeral comment on the heat. One complains that the sun is as oppressive as lead, while the other mentions that it has not been this hot in years. Martirio is the only woman who claims not to feel the heat (sexual frustration); but she later admits, along with Amelia and Magdalena, how bad the heat is for her, too. It is interesting to note that Lorca had the women assembled in the hot house, while the men are outside on the patio. Ostensibly, the men are there because Bernarda does not want them entering her house; figuratively, they are in the free world outside of the repression that reigns within Bernarda's private domain. Finally, those who are outside and free do not suffer from sexual oppression, i.e., heat.

In the same scene, La Poncia refers to another kind of heat—the warmth of a man's body, whose absence makes Bernarda the bitter person she is. By the second act, Martirio is willing to admit that she longs for November and its rains—anything but the heat of summer. There again is water imagery: the rain as a relief from frustration. The stallion referred to earlier tries to break out because it too is suffering from the heat. Bernarda uses the word *tormenta* (storm) to describe the turmoil in her house that can lead to the worst fate of all—a scandal.

Lorca also used techniques of sound and light and the symbolism attached to day and night. The most obvious use of sound and light techniques is in the third act of *Blood Wedding*. To create a surreal ambience, he specified a dark atmosphere and the sound of violins in the dark. With the appearance of the Beggar Woman (Death), the lights are lowered, and with the appearance of the Moon, whose job it is to provide light to find the victims, the lighting becomes intense. With the Moon's exit, the stage is again dark for the brutal acts of mutual murder. After the killings, the lighting turns blue.

Lorca set off the dream sequence that begins *Yerma* from the rest of the first act through the lighting. "La escena tiene una extraña luz de sueño." (1273; *The stage has a strange, dreamlike light*). After the stylized tiptoe walk across stage by the shepherd and the child, the scene changes to the "alegre luz de mañana de primavera" (1273; *happy light of a spring morning*). Every morning brings another chance for Yerma to become a part of the productive world. Only in the first act, when hope is strongest for Yerma, did Lorca specify that it is spring. There is a change in lighting in the scene between Yerma and Víctor. Just after Víctor announces that he will be moving, the stage falls into a soft shadow. There is no joy in the scene for Yerma, and there is no "joy" in the lighting. The play is, after all, written from Yerma's point of view. When Víctor finally takes his leave, the lighting reflects Yerma's spirits—almost obscure. As the Sisters-in-Law search for Yerma and call her name, the scene falls pitch-black. In addition, all the deaths take place in the dead of night.

There are a variety of lesser visual and gestural effects. In *Bernarda Alba,* the women parade into Bernarda's home after the funeral adorned with large handkerchiefs, skirts, and fans. In *Yerma,* the entrance of the shepherd and the child borders on ballet, as does the rhythmical washing sequence of the Washerwomen. In the scene at the fertility rite, young women run around with large ribbons in their hands. There are also the masks that the Male and the Female carry, not to mention the erotically symbolic horn that the Male carries and shakes at the Female. The surrealistic scene in *Blood Wedding* serves as spectacle as much as it does to further the story.

Aural effects abound. Sometimes they occur as voices singing and as the music of guitars, as in the wedding scene in *Blood Wedding;* the sounds of the eerie strains of the violins open and end the first scene of act 3. In *Yerma,* guitar music and hand clapping accompany the erotic song of the Male. In *The House of Bernarda Alba* the sound of church bells begins the play, followed shortly by the choral effect of the mourners reciting responsively the *Requiem.* There are the voices of the Reapers and, finally, Pepe's whistle. In each case, the sound is a key to the theme or meaning of the play. *Blood Wedding* has at its center a wedding; the sensual song in *Yerma* is what the play is all about; the song of the Reapers is about the sex and freedom for which the daughters and grandmother of *Bernarda Alba* long; and Pepe's whistle signals the kind of subservient relationship that exists between him and Adela.

Finally, there is the chorus in each play. The chorus commenting on the action of the play is an important element in Greek tragedy, and so it is in Lorca's tragic triolgy. Robert Lima and Luis González-del-Valle have already shown how the Woodcutters and the Girls in the third act of *Blood Wedding* serve the function of a chorus.[15] The Woodcutters comment on the flight of Leonardo and the Bride, and the Girls use images that relate to blood and death, *cuchillo* (knife) and *carmesí* (crimson): one is the tool of death, the other the color of blood. In *Yerma,* the chorus is composed of the Washerwomen, who show little pity for Yerma's plight. In *Bernarda Alba,* the neighbors in act 1 after the funeral serve as a chorus; Robert Hogan and Sven Molin have suggested that the sisters other than Adela also serve as a chorus commenting on the society within the household.[16]

Style: Techniques and Images

Two symbols of bad luck—and thus a foreboding about the future—appear in the scene with Prudencia: spilled salt and an engagement ring of pearls rather than diamonds. Amelia admonishes Magdalena for spilling salt; Magdalena cannot imagine her luck getting any worse than it is already. In addition, when Prudencia sees Angustias's engagement ring, she remarks that in her day pearls stood for tears. Adela is only too quick in seconding the neighbor's idea, despite Angustia's insistence that beliefs have changed. Finally, Bernarda intervenes by saying that things go the way one proposes (*"las cosas son como uno se las propone"* [1510]). Martirio reminds the family, *"O como Dios dispone* (1511; Or as God disposes). Before the act and the night are over, all the bad luck predicted in this scene comes to pass.

Conclusion

There are many reasons for reading plays, as there are for reading any other genre of literature. The first is for the pure enjoyment of the literary work. However, plays offer more than just fun and dramatic intensity: they are a glimpse of the cultures in which they take place. In the trilogy, for example, *Blood Wedding* shows the local customs of courtship and marriage. *Yerma* depicts the high premium that traditional Hispanic society places on having children. *The House of Bernarda Alba* portrays the circumscribed lives of unmarried women in Spanish towns. Small things, such as the role of sewing in the lives of Spanish women, become a thread running through the three plays. In *Blood Wedding*, one of the things the Mother looks forward to doing is adorning clothes for grandchildren; the first sight of Leonardo's wife is while she sits knitting; one of the Bride's "selling points" that her father mentions is her ability to sew. As *Yerma* opens, the character is asleep with the sewing basket at her feet. The activity that Bernarda has decided on for her daughters for the next eight years is embroidering their trousseaux. In fact, act 2 opens with the sisters sewing and asking whether or not to embroider Pepe's initials on Angustias's sheets.

All three plays depict relationships between men and women. The women's suffering and feelings of isolation are the consequences of men's actions and attitudes. In *Blood Wedding*, the Mother, the Wife, and the Bride are all left alone in their struggles against destiny after the Bridegroom and Leonardo have killed each other. Yerma's infecundity is a result of her husband's lack of desire to have a child. As

Angel del Río saw it, Yerma's plight is the "inability of the man to reciprocate the woman's passion" (137). Pepe el Romano is at the core of the immediate problems that affect Bernarda Alba's household. Del Río summed up the themes of the trilogy as "sexual obsession and unsatisfied love" (140).

All the plays involve physical searches. The Bridegroom pursues the Bride and Leonardo; the Sisters-in-Law search for Yerma as she goes to Dolores's house; Martirio knows that if she looks for Adela in the corral, she will find her there—and also see Pepe. The searches are all motivated by honor, jealousy, and revenge.

The trilogy represents responses to growing anxieties. In the three plays, there are three different attempts on the part of the women to free themselves from impossible situations. The frustrated Bride attempts to relieve her problems by running off with Leonardo. An anguished Yerma kills her husband. A hopeless Adela kills herself.

There are strong threads that bind the plays of the trilogy both thematically and technically, but in the final analysis they are all about the end of a genealogical line. The Mother of *Blood Wedding,* who yearns for grandchildren and is preoccupied with the perpetuation of her familial line, must spend the rest of her life knowing that when she dies so dies her bloodline. The situation of the grandmother in *The House of Bernarda Alba* is just as critical. Yerma will never see another generation: she herself kills off that possibility.

The masterpieces of drama that make up the tragic trilogy did not just happen. They are the culmination of Lorca's career as poet, playwright, director, composer, and visual artist. In fact, the elements of his mature works can be traced to the seeds that he planted and cultivated throughout his career. Suffering heroines do not appear for the first time in the tragic trilogy; they are characters in the puppet farces, in *Mariana Pineda,* and in *Rosie the Spinster,* the play that Lorca wrote between *Yerma* and *The House of Bernarda Alba.* Rosita, the pathetic, young bride in *Los títeres de cachiporra (The Billy Club Puppets),* is married to Cristobita because her father sold her off to the fat, hunchbacked, domineering tyrant. Her problem is the same as Yerma's: she had no chance to select a husband for herself. As one might expect, before her marriage Rosita supported her father by sewing.

The struggle for freedom, which culminates with Adela, begins in 1925 with Mariana Pineda, who goes to her death rather than betray her ideals or her lover. She is the victim of Pedrosa, an unprincipled and cold-blooded politician. Doña Rosita the spinster does not die in a physical sense at the end of the play but goes through life a lonely old maid because of a dishonest man who let her waste her youth believing that he was going to marry her; he was already married to another woman.[1] Even the Butterfly in *The Butterfly's Evil Spell* is left without the "man" she loves because he is more interested in pursuing a poetic ideal than he is in her. Strangely enough, Yerma's immediate predecessor who suffers pangs of frustrated parenthood is not another woman, but rather the *Joven* (Young Man) in *As Five Years Pass*. He is tormented by the thought that he might never become a father.

The sensual qualities of the Bride and Adela also begin in an early work, the one-act "*La doncella, el marinero y el estudiante*" ("The Maiden, the Sailor, and the Student"). The young woman is embroidering the initials of the men she desires; she includes most of the alphabet. Next there is Belisa, the young wife of the mature Perlimplín, in *Amor de don Perlimplín con Belisa en su jardín (The Love of Perlimplín with Belisa in the Garden)*. Like Adela, she is preoccupied with her body. She spends her wedding night entertaining men who represent the five races (all of mankind)—but not her husband. This might be a foreshadowing of the loveless wedding night in *Blood Wedding*. Finally, there is another Rosita, in *Retablillo de don Cristóbal (Christopher's Little Stage)*. She has fantasies of being

> *en el diván*
> *con Juan,*
> *en el colchón*
> *con Ramón,*
> *en el canapé*
> *con José*
> *en la silla*
> *con Medinilla,*

en el suelo
con el que yo quiero,
pegada al muro
con el lindo Arturo,
y en la gran "chaise-longue"
con Juan, con José, con Medinilla,
con Arturo y con Ramón.
(1032)

(on the divan
with Juan,
on the mattress
with Ramón,
on the sofa
with José
on the chair
with Medinilla,
on the floor
with the one I want,
against the wall
with handsome Arturo,
and on the chaise lounge
with Juan, José, Medinilla,
Arturo and Ramón.)

Edwin Honig concluded that "the poet, identified with all his heroines, perpetuates desire endlessly in an eroticism which, like Yerma's, ends in a metaphorical suicide, or like Dona Rosita's [la soltera], spreads itself through the fields and wells and walls of Granada's circumambiance."[2] The men in Lorca's plays have received considerably less attention than the women because they are often secondary characters and less interesting than their feminine counterparts.

Lorca's interest in children as characters began in *Mariana Pineda,* a dramatization of a traditional childhood song, written as a child might have dreamed it.[3] The Child (*Niña*) who has the dream is one of the little girls who sing the ballad of Mariana Pineda in the play's prologue. The Child then provides the key for understanding the play, for it is she who is dreaming the sentimental and melodramatic details of which the play is composed.

Conclusion

Lorca used children as messengers of truth. For example, the *Child* (*Niño*) in *The Shoemaker's Prodigious Wife* is the only person in the whole town who can understand the Shoemaker's Wife (*Zapatera*) and sympathize with her. He serves as a counterpoint of tenderness and compassion in contrast to the violence and ridicule of the members of society against whom she struggles. The Child is the one person who is on the Shoemaker's Wife's side and who keeps her abreast of what the town is saying about her. Just as there are Christological associations in the character of the Child who appears at the beginning of *Yerma*, so there are in this play. When the Child asks the Shoemaker's Wife who he is, she calls him "*pastorcillo de Belén*" (943; little shepherd from Bethlehem). There is an important reference to a child in the collection *Poet in New York*. Lorca ended the poem "*Oda a Walt Whitman*" with the lines,

> *Quiero que el aire fuerte de la noche más honda*
> *quite flores y letras del arco donde duermes*
> *y un niño negro anuncie a los blancos del oro*
> *la llegada del reino de la espiga.*
> (526)

> I want the strong air of deepest night
> to take away the flowers and letters of the archway where you are
>   sleeping
> and a black child to announce to the whites of the gold
> the arrival of the kingdom of the spike of grain.)

In other words, Lorca saw a child as the one who would announce the new period in history, when peaceful vegetation will have dominance over money and other tools of dehumanization. That child will be the savior of the world.

The image of the horse has deep roots in Lorca's plays and poems. References here will be limited to the plays. The one-act "*Quimera*" ("Chimera"), a very short play, has four characters: Enrique, the *Mujer* (Wife), the *Viejo* (Old Man), and the *Niña* (Young Girl). The Old Man, who was once a coachman for Enrique's wife, confesses, "*Nadie sabe el miedo que a mí me dan los caballos. Caiga un rayo sobre todos sus ojos. . . . ¡Malditos sean los caballos!"* (905; Nobody knows how afraid I am of horses. May lightning strike their eyes. . . . Damn all horses!). He wants to know if the six children who are calling from the house are Enrique's; when he learns that they are, he remembers that *"ella [Mujer] no tenía miedo a los caballos. Ella es feliz"* (905; she [the Wife] was never afraid of horses. She's happy). In that statement, he establishes the relationship between a person who is not afraid of horses and one who is fulfilled and has children.

In *The Shoemaker's Prodigious Wife,* the Shoemaker's Wife remembers her former lover in his pose on a horse. *"Pero el que me gustaba a mí de todos era Emiliano . . . que venía montado en una jaca negra"* (917; But the one I liked of all of them was Emiliano . . . who used to come mounted on a black jennet). When the old Shoemaker can take no more of his wife's nagging, he leaves her; in his absence, she idealizes her lackluster husband: *"Yo me miraba en sus ojos. Cuando le veía venir montado en su jaca blanca . . . me miró y lo miré. . . . El paró su caballo y la cola del caballo era blanca y tan larga que llegaba al agua del arroyo"* (945–46; I would look at myself in his eyes. When I used to see him come mounted on his white jennet . . . he looked at me and I looked at him. . . . He stopped his horse and its tail was white and so long that it reached to the water of the arroyo). The Child, to whom she reminisces, finds it hard to believe that the Shoemaker ever had a horse—that is to say, that he was ever young, vigorous, and virile.

In *El público (The Audience),* horses are sexual aggressors in a setting with women, as well as the passive objects of desire of the male character of the Director. In the play's first scene, the Director tells the audience in an aside that *"Ya se ha inventado la cama para dormir con los caballos"* (The bed was invented in order to sleep with horses).[4] In the third scene of the same work, there is the unconventional production of *Romeo and Juliet* in which men play the two main roles. Caballo Blanco I (White Horse I) approaches Juliet and makes romantic overtures toward her. The horse is taking the place of Romeo, the archetypal romantic hero in Western literature. One of Lorca's purposes in this play was to depict amorous/sexual relationships, which were frowned upon in his native Spain of the 1930s. His message seems to be that love exists with equal intensity on numerous levels, and that one manifestation is no better or worse than any other. At the time of Lorca's death, he had not yet completed all the plays for which he had outlines. One of them was to be "*El hombre y la jaca*" (The man and the horse) in which a boy is in love with his horse.[5]

This study has been using the word *tragedy* rather loosely, not in a strictly Aristotelian sense. Chapter 4 showed that Lorca was often true to the spirit of tragedy without rigorously applying the rules of the Greek master. None of the plays transpires within a chronological period of 24 hours. Only *The House of Bernarda Alba* more or less observes the unity of place: while the drama takes place within a single house, each act is set in a different room. There is some observance of the unity of action. *Blood Wedding* focuses on the Bridegroom-Bride-Leonardo triangle, with additional attention to the plight of the Mother, who harbors hatred and resentment of Leonardo's family and loses her last son. (One could argue that the play is about the Mother, and that the wedding is the means by which she loses her son.) *Yerma* is exclusively about the anguish of the title character.[6] *The House of Bernarda Alba* is episodic but true to the theme of amorous/sexual frustration.

Lorca's breaking of the unities is consistent with the history of Spanish theater. Félix Lope de Vega, the "father" of Spanish drama during the Golden Age, established non-Aristotelian rules for Spain's dramatists. (See the Bibliography for studies that focus on the tragic dimension of the plays.) From the tense opening scenes, through the tragic climaxes, disharmony reigns on every level of Lorca's plays. As María Teresa Babín viewed it, "Lorca's theater expresses in poetry the states of agony of the spirit."[7] Lorca wanted theater to be poetry that jumps off the page and becomes human. He believed that the theater had to capture the drama of contemporary life and inspire passion in the audience, as classical drama did. He considered theater a barometer of society, a way of measuring a country's greatness. He believed in the power of theater to develop sensitivity and to change society.

Lorca's trilogy is the work of a total artist and a committed human being. He brought to his mature works his experience in poetry, painting, and music, as well as his experiences in every realm of theater—play writing, directing, and even costume designing. His characters and insights come from his extensive travels around his native land. His themes reflect his compassion.

Lorca is one of those rare writers who are so good that it is worth the trouble of learning the language in which they wrote to be able to read their original texts. To open the first page of a play by Lorca is to pass through a one-way door. No other Spanish playwright provides the same poetic and dramatic satisfaction he does. Lorca began the last stanza of his lament for Ignacio Sánchez Mejías with the lines:

> *Tardará mucho tiempo en nacer, si es que nace,*
> *un andaluz tan claro, tan rico de aventura. (545)*

> (He will be a long time in coming, if ever he is born,
> an Andalusian so sparkling, so rich in adventure.)

The words not only praised his friend, they were prophetic about himself.

Notes and References

Chapter 2

1. 24 June 1989. All translations of quoted material are my own and have been made with concern for conveying the meaning of the citation. I have generally not included in brackets those words that I have supplied for syntactical reasons or for elucidating the sense of the quotation.

Chapter 3

1. 9 March 1933.
2. Signed only A.C., 9 March 1933.
3. *New York World-Telegram*, 12 February 1935.
4. *New York Times*, 12 February 1935.
5. *New York Herald Tribune*, 12 February 1935.
6. *New York American*, 12 February 1935.
7. *New York Daily News*, 12 February 1935.
8. *New York Sun*, 12 February 1935.
9. *Palo Alto* (Calif.) *Times*, 27 December 1952.
10. *New York Journal-American*, 1 April 1958.
11. *New York Times*, 1 April 1958.
12. *New York Times*, 3 June 1980.
13. *Cleveland Plain Dealer*, 10 October 1988.
14. *Miami Herald*, 9 December 1988.
15. Ibid.
16. Ibid.
17. *Miami Herald*, 10 December 1988.
18. "*Federico García Lorca y la tragedia*" (Federico García Lorca and tragedy), interview with Juan Chabas, in Federico García Lorca, *Obras com-*

pletas (Complete Works), 15th ed. (Madrid: Aguilar, 1969). All material quoted from the plays (except for excerpts from *The Audience*) are from this edition. Page numbers appear in the text, and translations are my own.

19. *La Voz* (The Voice), 31 December 1934.

20. Signed A.C., 30 December 1934.

21. *La Epoca* (The Epoch), 31 December 1934.

22. *Diario universal* (Universal Daily), 31 December 1934.

23. *Ahora* (Now), 31 December 1934.

24. *Revista cubana* (Cuban Review) 1 (February–March 1935), 266–69.

25. Rosa Schneider, "*Acotaciones al margen de* Yerma *de García Lorca*" ("Marginal Notes on García Lorca's *Yerma*"), *Claridad* (Clarity) 16, no. 315 (July 1937), n. p.

26. George Freedley, 27 December 1947.

27. *Philadelphia Inquirer,* 18 December 1966.

28. *Newark [N.J.] Evening News,* 9 December 1966.

29. Norman Nadel, 9 December 1966.

30. Michael Smith, 22 December 1966.

31. *New Yorker,* 28 October 1972, 119, 120.

32. 26 October 1972.

33. *Saturday Review,* 11 November 1972, 80.

34. Unsigned, 13 November 1972.

35. *Women's Wear Daily,* 19 October 1972.

36. *Sur* (South) 126 (April 1945), 59–61.

37. 9 March 1945.

38. Vol. 3, no. 10 (June 1945), 1.

39. 7 June 1960.

40. *San Francisco Examiner,* 17 September 1963.

41. 11 January 1964.

42. *New York Times,* 28 February 1972.

43. Edward Moran, 21 November 1974.

44. Richard F. Shepard, *New York Times,* 23 November 1979.

45. 29 May 1989.

Chapter 4

1. I am not using the words *tragic* and *tragedy* in this book in an Aristotelian sense, but rather in a Lorquian sense. Whether or not Lorca's plays fulfill every requirement set forth by the great Greek philosopher, they do depict suffering and end in death.

2. Spanish has two words for *scene: cuadro* and *escena*. A *cuadro* is a larger division than an *escena;* the former indicates a change of set, while the latter indicates a change of characters within the same setting. The three acts of *Blood Wedding* are subdivided into seven *cuadros,* as those of *Yerma* are divided into six *cuadros.* For *Bernarda Alba,* I use the word *scene* to indicate a change of characters within each act.

3. It is worth noting now (and explaining why later in the text) that Leonardo is the only character in the play with a proper name and the only one not described in terms of his relationship to another character, such as the Mother or the Bridegroom.

4. Lorca wrote *Rosie the Spinster* in 1935 between *Yerma* and *The House of Bernarda Alba.* While it does not form part of the trilogy, it is a forerunner of *Bernarda Alba* in its characterization of young women who are obsessed with the idea of marriage. In one interview, Lorca referred to *Doña Rosita* as a sordid drama on the problem of being a spinster in Spain. He thought of it as a simple, amiable, bourgeois work that gave him a rest from tragedy after having written *Blood Wedding* and *Yerma* (1763).

Chapter 5

1. For a study of the male characters, see Dennis A. Klein, "The Development of the Male Character in the Theatre of Federico García Lorca," *García Lorca Review* 5 (1977), 81–94.

2. For a complete study of this aspect of the play, see Dennis A. Klein, "Christological Imagery in Lorca's *Yerma,*" *García Lorca Review* 6 (1978), 35–42.

3. See, too, Robert E. Lott, "*Yerma:* The Tragedy of Unjust Barrenness," *Modern Drama* 8 (1965), 20–27.

4. John V. Falconieri focuses on Juan's plight in "Tragic Hero in Search of a Role: *Yerma*'s Juan," *Revista de estudios hispánicos* (Journal of Hispanic studies) 1 (1967), 17–33.

5. "*The House of Bernarda Alba:* A Director's Notes and Afterthoughts," *Drama Critique* 9, no. 2 (Spring 1966), 86.

Chapter 6

1. For further reading on the subject of women as victims of male-dominated Andalusian society and of each other in Lorca's plays, see Julianne Burton, "The Greatest Punishment: Female and Male in Lorca's Tragedies," in *Women in Hispanic Literature: Icons and Fallen Idols,* ed. Beth Miller, 259–79 (Berkeley: University of California Press, 1963); and Sumner M. Green-

field, "Yerma, the Woman and the Work: Some Reconsiderations," *Estreno* (Opening night) 7, no. 1 (Spring 1981), 18–21.

2. Angel del Río states, "Here is the basic element of the tragedy: persons consumed by deep passion, against which it is useless to fight." In *Vida y obras de Federico García Lorca* (The life and works of Federico García Lorca) (Zaragoza, Spain: Heraldo de Aragón, 1952), 131.

3. Lorca used as the basis for his play a newspaper account of a bride who ran off with her lover on the day of her wedding; a duel followed between the husband and the lover.

Chapter 7

1. See Gustavo Correa, "*El simbolismo de la luna en la poesía de García Lorca*" (The symbolism of the moon in the poetry of García Lorca), *PMLA* 72 (1957), 1060–84, for his interpretation of this detail of the play.

2. Del Río quotes the 10 April 1938 issue of the Cuban newspaper *Carteles* (Billboard): Lorca wanted his new play to have "*¡Ni una gota de poesía! ¡Realidad! ¡Realismo!*" (Not a drop of poetry! Reality! Realism!), 141–42.

3. A review signed "Cahn" in *Variety* (29 November 1972, 62) calls Yerma an Everywoman, struggling against a fate that her world decrees inevitable.

4. For notes on the names Angustias and Martirio, see Grace Alvarez-Altman, "*Nihilismo sexual en* La casa de Bernarda Alba" (Sexual nihilism in *The House of Bernarda Alba*), *García Lorca Review* 3 (1975), 67–69.

5. One might wonder about why Bernarda's last name is Alba and not Benavides. In Spanish society, the proper title for a widow would include her late husband's last name; Bernarda's name would be Viuda de Benavides (Widow of Benavides). A possible explanation is the fact that Lorca wanted the symbolism of the word for *white* in the name *Alba*, as suggested to me by Prof. Sumner M. Greenfield. Another explanation is that the real-life family on which the play is modeled was named Alba. For details about that family, see Miguel García-Posada, "*Realidad y transfiguración artística en* La casa de Bernarda Alba" (Reality and artistic transfiguration in *The House of Bernarda Alba*), in La casa de Bernarda Alba *y el teatro de García Lorca* (*The House of Bernarda Alba* and the theater of García Lorca), ed. Ricardo Doménech, 158–59 (Madrid: Cátedra, 1985).

6. The text of his talk is in *Obras completas* under the title "*Las nanas infantiles*" (Children's lullabies), 91–108.

7. For comments on the inherent poetic quality of the play, see Sumner M. Greenfield, "Poetry and Stagecraft in *La casa de Bernarda Alba*," *Hispania* 38 (1955), 456–61.

Notes and References

8. "The Poet in Dublin," in *In Search of Theatre* (New York: Alfred A. Knopf, 1953), 215–32.

9. See also Vicente Cabrera, "Poetic Structure in Lorca's *La casa de Bernarda Alba*," *Hispania* 61 (1978), 466–71.

10. For a thorough and systematic study of Lorca's imagery, see Concha Zardoya, "*La técnica metafórica de Federico García Lorca*" (The metaphoric technique of Federico García Lorca), *Revista hispánica moderna* 20, no. 4 (October 1954), 295–326.

11. See further discussion in Julian Palley, "Archetypal Symbols in *Bodas de sangre*," *Hispania* 50 (1967), 74–79.

12. For further comments on the horses, see Rafael Martínez Nadal, El público: *Amor, teatro y caballos en la obra de Federico García Lorca* (The audience: love, theater, and horses in the work of Federico García Lorca) (Oxford: Dolphin, 1970); and Juan Villegas, "*El leitmotiv del caballo en* Bodas de sangre" (The leitmotiv of the horse in *Blood Wedding*), *Hispanófila* 29 (1967), 21–36.

13. For more information on floral symbolism in Lorca's plays, see Luis González-del-Valle, *La tragedia en el teatro de Unamuno, Valle-Inclán y García Lorca* (Tragedy in the theater of Unamuno, Valle-Inclán, and García Lorca) (New York: Eliseo Torres and Sons, 1975).

14. *The New Testament,* New International Version (New York: New York Bible Society International, 1973).

15. Robert Lima, *The Theatre of García Lorca* (New York: Las Américas, 1963), 207; Luis González-del-Valle, "*Bodas de sangre y sus elementos trágicos*" (*Blood Wedding* and its tragic elements), *Archivum* (Universidad de Oviedo) 21 (1971), 114.

16. See *Drama: The Major Genres* (New York: Dodd, Mead and Co., 1966), 191; and Cabrera, "Poetic Structure in Lorca's *La casa de Bernarda Alba*."

Conclusion

1. For details, see Frances Colecchia, "*Doña Rosita—una heroína aparte*" (Doña Rosita—a heroine apart), *Duquesne Hispanic Review* 7, no. 2 (1968), 37–43.

2. *García Lorca* (Norfolk, Conn.: New Directions, 1963), 196.

3. See Sumner M. Greenfield, "The Problem of *Mariana Pineda*," *Massachusetts Review* 1 (1960), 751–63.

4. Federico García Lorca, El público y Comedia sin título: *Dos obras póstumas,* ed. Rafael Martínez Nadal and Marie Laffranque, (Barcelona: Seix Barral, 1978), 35.

5. For information about this unfinished work, see Manuel Altolaguirre, "*Nuestro teatro*" (Our theater), *Hora de España* (The Spanish hour) 9 (1937), 29–37. For information on Lorca's other incomplete projects, see Marie Laffranque, "Federico García Lorca: Teatro abierto. Teatro inconcluso" (Federico García Lorca: open theater, unfinished theater), in Doménech, La casa de Bernarda Alba *y el teatro de García Lorca,* 213–30.

6. See Calvin Cannon, "*Yerma* as Tragedy," *Symposium* 16, no. 2 (Summer 1962), 85–93.

7. *García Lorca: Vida y obra* (García Lorca: life and work) (New York: Las Américas, 1955), 33.

Selected Bibliography

Lorca's works appear in numerous editions, both in Spanish and in translation. I am including here only the Spanish edition of Lorca's complete works. References on translations appear in Colecchia's *Primary Bibliography,* listed below. The present bibliography is limited to studies of Lorca's theater (some are "life and works") and does not include exclusively biographical works.

Primary Works

Obras completas (Complete works), 15th ed. Madrid: Aguilar, 1969. Contains the texts of Lorca's poetry, plays, prose, speeches and interviews, and correspondence. (The 22d edition was published in 1986.)

Three Tragedies of Federico García Lorca. Translated by James Graham-Luján and Richard O'Connell. New York: New Directions, 1955. The most commonly used translation of the trilogy.

El público y Comedia sin título: *Dos obras póstumas.* ed. Rafael Martínez Nadal and Marie Laffranque. Barcelona: Seix Barral, 1978. The text of the two plays (*The Audience* and *Untitled Play*) in as complete a form as is currently available. On facing pages are the original manuscript (in typed form) and the edited text. Preliminary note by Martínez Nadal and prologue by the editors.

Secondary Works

Books

Babín, María Teresa. *García Lorca: Vida y obra* (García Lorca: life and work). New York: Las Américas, 1955. Thematic rather than chronological presentation of the works—theater, poetry, and prose.

Berenguer Carisomo, Arturo. *Las máscaras de Federico García Lorca* (The masks of Federico García Lorca). Buenos Aires, 1941. Relates the individual works to each other and to Spanish literature on a broad scale. Traces Lorca's poetic roots back to the Spanish poetry of the Middle Ages and the Golden Age.

Cuadernos hispanoamericanos (Hispano-American notebooks) dedicated four numbers to Lorquian studies on the occasion of the fiftieth anniversary of his death. Several of the articles in nos. 433–34 (July–August 1986) are on Lorca's plays.

Doménech, Ricardo, ed. La casa de Bernarda Alba *y el teatro de García Lorca* (*The House of Bernarda Alba* and the theater of García Lorca). Madrid: Cátedra, 1985. A collection of essays by diverse critics. Most of the studies are on *The House of Bernarda Alba.*

González-del-Valle, Luis. *La tragedia en el teatro de Unamuno, Valle-Inclán y García Lorca* (Tragedy in the theater of Unamuno, Valle-Inclán, and García Lorca). New York: Eliseo Torres and Sons, 1975. Useful for a treatment of the tragic elements in Lorca.

Lima, Robert. *The Theater of García Lorca.* New York: Las Américas, 1963. A critical study in English of all of Lorca's plays available in print at the time of its writing.

Londré, Felicia Hardison. *Federico García Lorca.* New York: Ungar, 1984. A study that integrates Lorca's talents as writer, artist, and musician. Text, in English, is the work of a dramaturge.

Machado Bonet, Ofelia. *Federico García Lorca: su producción dramática.* Montevideo, 1951. A chronological presentation of Lorca's theater with a chapter on each play except *Teatro breve* (*Short Plays*) and *Cachiporra* (*The Billy Club Puppets*).

Martínez Nadal, Rafael. El público: *Amor, teatro y caballos en la obra de Federico García Lorca* (The audience: love, theater, and horses in the works of Federico García Lorca). Oxford: Dolphin, 1970. A study in two parts: the first is on *The Audience;* the second is on love, horses, and theater-within-the-theater in Lorca's plays.

Nourissier, François. *F. García Lorca, dramaturge.* Paris: L'Arche, 1955. Views Lorca's plays as examples of "total theater"—spectacle, poetry, song, dance, and costume. Text in French.

Selected Bibliography

Articles

The Trilogy

Alberich, J. "*El erotismo femenino en el teatro de García Lorca*" (Feminine eroticism in the theater of García Lorca). *Papeles de Son Armadans* (Papers from Son Armadans) 38–39 (1965), 9–36. A Freudian study of the women in the three tragedies.

Babín, María Teresa. "*La mujer en la obra de García Lorca*" (Women in the work of García Lorca). *La Torre* 9 (1961), 125–37. An analysis of the feminine characters in Lorca's plays.

Blanco-González, Manuel. "Lorca: The Tragic Trilogy." *Drama Critique* 9, no. 2 (1966), 91–97. Some statements are accurate, others are exaggerated, and much of the information has been said before; but provides a good analysis for students more comfortable reading in English than in Spanish.

Burton, Julianne. "Earth, Air, Fire, and Water: Imagery and Symbols in the Tragedies of Federico García Lorca." *García Lorca Review* 3 (1975), 99–120. Treats the pertinent imagery in the three tragedies.

Carbonell Basset, Delfín. "*Tres dramas existenciales de F. García Lorca*" (Three existential dramas of F. García Lorca). *Cuadernos hispanoamericanos* 190 (1965), 118–30. Applies Heidegger's philosophy of existence to the Bride, Yerma, and Adela.

Carrier, Warren. "Poetry in the Drama of Lorca." *Drama Survey* 2, no. 3 (1963), 297–304. Treats *Mariana Pineda* as well as the plays of the trilogy in its exploration and explanation of the poetic elements of the plays.

Correa, Gustavo. "*El simbolismo de la luna en la poesía de García Lorca*" (The symbolism of the moon in the poetry of García Lorca). *PMLA* 72 (1957), 1060–84. Discusses the symbol of the moon in *Bodas de sangre* (*Blood Wedding*) and *Yerma* as well as in *Así que pasen cinco años* (*As Five Years Pass*) and Lorca's poetry.

González-Gerth, Miguel. "The Tragic Symbolism of Federico García Lorca." *Texas Quarterly* 13, no. 2 (1970), 56–63. Discusses the image of blood in the trilogy and other plays.

Greenfield, Sumner M. "Lorca's Theatre: A Synthetic Reexamination." *Journal of Spanish Studies: Twentieth Century* 5, no. 1 (Spring 1977), 31–46. On the fundamental nature of Lorca's theater, which for the playwright was "a poetic event of stylized theatricality with its own artistic integrity."

———. "Lorca's Tragedies: Practice without Theory." *Siglo XX/20th Century* 4, nos. 1 and 2 (1986–87), 1–5. Begins with the premise that Lorca wrote his trilogy with no preconceived, theoretic notions. Analyzes the plays as tragedies—Lorquian if not Aristotelian.

Klein, Dennis A. "Children in the Theatre of Federico García Lorca." *García Lorca Review* 7 (1979), 109–18. The roles of children in Lorca's plays.

――――. "The Development of the Male Character in the Theatre of Federico García Lorca." *García Lorca Review* 5 (1977), 81–94. Traces the masculine characters through Lorca's various periods of dramas.

――――. "*El maleficio de la mariposa:* The Cornerstone of García Lorca's Theatre." *García Lorca Review* 2 (1974), n. p. Shows how the character types in Lorca's earliest play developed into the characters in the trilogy.

――――. "The Old Women in the Theater of García Lorca." *García Lorca Review* 3 (1975), 91–98. Treats the Maid in *Blood Wedding,* the Old Woman in *Yerma,* and María Josefa in *The House of Bernarda Alba.*

Rees, Margaret A. "'Rosa y jazmín de Granada': The Role of Flowers in Lorca's Plays and Poetry." In *Leeds Papers on Lorca and on Civil War Verse,* ed. Margaret A. Rees, 81–91. Leeds, England: Trinity and All Saints' College, 1988. Interpretation of floral imagery in the tragedies.

Zardoya, Concha. "*La técnica metafórica de Federico García Lorca*" (The metaphoric technique of Federico García Lorca). *Revista hispánica moderna* 20, no. 4 (October 1954), 295–326. A thorough and systematic study of Lorca's imagery.

Blood Wedding

Barnes, Robert. "The Fusion of Poetry and Drama in *Blood Wedding.*" *Modern Drama* 2 (1960), 395–402. Pays considerable attention to color symbolism and to the visual aspects of the play. The attitude ascribed to the Bride is questionable; the rest of the article is carefully considered.

González-del-Valle, Luis. "Bodas de sangre *y sus elementos trágicos*" (*Blood Wedding* and its tragic elements). *Archivum* (Universidad de Oviedo) 21 (1971), 95–120. Treats Aristotelian elements in the play.

――――. "*Justicia poética en* Bodas de sangre" (Poetic justice in *Blood Wedding*). *Romance Notes* 14 (1972), 236–41. Discusses tragic flaws in the characters of the Mother, the Bride, and the Bridegroom and other elements that make the play a tragedy.

Halliburton, Charles Lloyd. "García Lorca, the Tragedian: An Aristotelian Analysis of *Bodas de sangre.*" *Revista de estudios hispánicos* (Journal of Hispanic studies) 2 (1968), 35–40. Applies Aristotelian terminology in an attempt to see if the play is truly a tragedy in the classical sense of the word.

López, Daniel. "Predestination in Federico García Lorca's *Bodas de sangre.*" *García Lorca Review* 5 (1977), 95–103.

Miller, Norman C. "Lullaby, Wedding Song, and Funeral Chant in García Lorca's *Bodas de sangre.*" *Gestos: Teoría y práctica del teatro hispánico*

Selected Bibliography

(Gestures: theory and practice in Hispanic theater) 3, no. 5 (April 1988), 41–51. Analyzes the three songs.

Touster, Eva K. "Thematic Patterns in Lorca's *Blood Wedding*." *Modern Drama* 7 (1964), 16–27. Studies the structure, symbols, and musical motifs in the play.

Villegas, Juan. "*El leitmotiv del caballo en* Bodas de sangre" (The leitmotiv of the horse in *Blood Wedding*). *Hispanófila* 29 (1967), 21–36. Study of the symbolic value of the horse.

Yerma

Cannon, Calvin. "The Imagery of Lorca's *Yerma*." *Modern Language Quarterly* 21, no. 2 (June 1960), 122–30. Interprets the images in the play and shows how they serve to express the play's fundamental tragic tension.

———. "*Yerma* as Tragedy." *Symposium* 16, no. 2 (Summer 1962), 85–93. A brilliant article that examines the plays of the trilogy and determines that of the three only *Yerma* is truly a tragedy.

Correa, Gustavo. "Honor, Blood and Poetry in *Yerma*." *Tulane Drama Review* 7 (1962), 96–110. (Translation by Rupert C. Allen, Jr., "Yerma," *Revista de las Indias* [Bogota] 35, no. 109 [1940], 11–63.) Supplies cultural information helpful in understanding Yerma's obsession with motherhood.

Falconieri, John V. "Tragic Hero in Search of a Role: *Yerma*'s Juan." *Revista de estudios hispánicos* (Journal of Spanish studies) 1 (1967), 17–33. An attempt to prove that it is Juan who is the tragic hero of the play.

Fernández-Cifuentes, Luis. "Yerma: Anatomy of a Transgression." *Modern Language Notes* 99 (1984), 288–307. Yerma's transgression is her obsession with motherhood. Good bibliography on the play's first production.

Greenfield, Sumner M. "Yerma, the Woman and the Work: Some Reconsiderations." *Estreno* 7, no. 1 (Spring 1981), 18–21. The play as a dramatic crescendo of the passing of time and women as the victims of a miscarriage of justice.

Klein, Dennis A. "Christological Imagery in Lorca's *Yerma*." *García Lorca Review* 6 (1978), 35–42. Treats imagery from the Gospels in the play.

Lott, Robert E. "*Yerma:* The Tragedy of Unjust Barrenness." *Modern Drama* 8 (1965), 20–27. Yerma, her society, and why the character's barrenness is so unfair.

Martínez Lacalle, Guadalupe. "*Yerma:* Una tragedia pura y simplemente." (*Yerma:* a tragedy pure and simple). *Neophilologus* (Groningen, Neth.) 72 (1988), 227–37. Approaches play on Lorquian and Aristotelian terms.

Skloot, Robert. "Theme and Image in Lorca's *Yerma*." *Drama Survey* 5 (1961), 151–61. The problem in the play is not just Yerma's barren state but also her code of honor, which the critic considers her flaw.

The House of Bernarda Alba

Arce de Vázquez, Margot. "*La casa de Bernarda Alba.*" *Sin nombre* (No name) 1, no. 2 (1970), 5–14. Treats structure, characterization, and stagecraft. Shows how Lorca presents the dramatic situation from all points of view—those of Bernarda, the servants, the neighbors, María Josefa, and each daughter.

Bentley, Eric. "The Poet in Dublin." In *In Search of Theatre*, 215–32. New York: Alfred A. Knopf, 1953. The fruits of the director's experience after staging *Bernarda Alba* at the Abbey Theatre. Dual point of view of a director and a literary critic.

Cabrera, Vicente. "Poetic Structure in Lorca's *La casa de Bernarda Alba.*" *Hispania* 61 (1978), 466–71. Discusses *Bernarda Alba* as poetic drama and the symbolic and structural elements of the play.

Cueto, Ronald. "On the Queerness Rampant in *The House of Bernarda Alba.*" In *Leeds Papers on Lorca and on Civil War Verse*, ed. Rees, 9–42. Examines onomastics in the play.

Greenfield, Sumner M. "Poetry and Stagecraft in *La casa de Bernarda Alba.*" *Hispania* 38 (1955), 456–61. Analyzes the symbolism in and poetic conception of the play. Discovers the poetry "of the theater" in a play written almost entirely in prose.

Bibliographies

Colecchia, Francesca, ed. *García Lorca: An Annotated Primary Bibliography.* New York: Garland Publishing, 1982. Includes an extensive bibliography of editions of Lorca's works in Spanish as well as in 24 other languages.

———, ed. *García Lorca: A Selectively Annotated Bibliography of Criticism.* New York: Garland Publishing, 1979. Contains a bibliography of scholarship about Lorca's plays.

Klein, Dennis A. "A Critical Bibliography of the Theatre of Federico García Lorca: 1940 through 1970." Unpublished doctoral dissertation, University of Massachusetts, 1973. Contains sections listing scholarly books and articles on Lorca's theater.

The *International Bibliography*, published annually by the Modern Language Association, is the best source of information on current literary scholarship.

Index

Index

The Author

Dennis A. Klein is professor of Spanish at the University of South Dakota. He received his B.S.E. and M.A. from the University of Kansas and his Ph.D., with a dissertation on García Lorca, from the University of Massachusetts. His writings on Hispanic and British drama have appeared in a wide variety of books and journals. He is a member of the committee that annually compiles the Modern Language Association's *International Bibliography* and has served as contributing editor for *García Lorca: A Selectively Annotated Bibliography of Criticism* and *García Lorca: An Annotated Primary Bibliography*, both edited by Francesca Colecchia.

Gramley Library
Salem College
Winston-Salem, NC 27108

Gramley Library
Salem College
Winston-Salem, NC 27108